BOOM TOWN REFLECTIONS

VOLUME – 5

LOST INNOCENCE

By

Mark A. Gregg

An Imprint of Collins Publishing House

4900 California Ave, Bakersfield, CA 93309, USA

Collins's website address: www.collinspublishinghouse.com

First published in English by Collins Publishing House in 2024

1st Edition 2024

Mark A. Gregg © 2024

Mark A. Gregg asserts the moral right

to be identified as the author of this work.

A catalogue record for this book is available

from the Library of Congress United States.

LCCN: 2024924237

E Book ISBN: 978-1-966029-34-2

Paperback ISBN: : 978-1-966029-35-9

Hardcover ISBN: 978-1-966029-36-6

Printed and bounded in United States of America.

For permission requests, contact
info@collinspublishinghouse.com

This book is dedicated to the memory of Pastor's Gordon and Lois Nelson. You both had a major, positive impact on our lives and we will always be thankful for this.

Table of Contents

CHAPTER 1
THE KANSAS DREAM

Technically, I should not be here writing this. I was supposed to die in a fiery plane crash with my wife and children. *No, I am not joking.*

After a series of prophetic dreams that all transpired *precisely* as revealed in my dreamscape, I had a 'final' dream of Vangie, Brandi, Brittanie, and I flying back from our vacation in Orlando, Florida and dying in a horrific plane crash. Every part of this dream transpired *exactly* as it was shown a few months prior, except, of course, the plane did not crash.

I still don't understand why the dream proceeded with perfect accuracy right up to the final part, where we were supposed to meet Christ when the plane crashed. *I still feel like it was a test.*

Returning to our home in Wheatland, Wyoming from our Disney World vacation meant a return to shift work and the humdrum of daily existence in windy Wyoming. Cheyenne and Fort Collins continued to be our respite from the mundane while First Assembly of God Church kept us busy on the weekends. Church continued to be good, and I enjoyed the worship (song) services more than ever.

The fact that we made it back alive from our Disney World trip changed my perspective about many things. For one, I was far more cognizant of the presence of the Lord in my life. Every thought, every decision, and everything I did was focused on what I should be doing in the light of His presence. I know the previous statement makes me sound very *"Churchy,"* but I can promise you that it was deeper than this.

Christ was now interwoven with my every thought and emotion. You either understand this, or you ridicule what happened passing it off as self-generated bluster. I can assure you the dreams were real and happened exactly as I wrote them. Interestingly, it turns out the dreams weren't finished yet.

Several weeks after returning from Disneyworld I had what appeared to be *another* prophetic dream. The format was the same as the previous ones. In this dream I saw myself getting to the plant, parking my car, and heading for the Shift Supervisor's office. As I walked into the admin building on my way to the shift office the janitor in the admin building stopped me to ask a question.

His name was Tommy Sawyer. He was a very short, portly, round-faced, curmudgeonly man with tight, dark, curly hair precipitously receding due to serious male pattern baldness. While curmudgeonly, he was probably not much older than me.

He spoke with a screechy, high-pitched voice, forming words in his throat more than his lips. The gossip in the plant was that he still lived with his mother even though he was making decent money working at the plant. I had never talked to him other than exchanging greetings on a few different occasions. In my dream he had a specific question for me.

"Hi!" His almost squeaky voice was grating. "Do you live in a white and black house on Elm Street?" He was leaning against the handle of his large dust mop and had his head cocked to one side. His eyes were poorly aligned, so he tended to always have one eye looking away from you. It was uncomfortable for me because I wasn't sure which eye to look at when talking to him.

I stopped to answer him. "Yes, why do you ask?"

"I was just wondering. It looked like your car in the driveway the other day." He had obviously driven into the cul-de-sac where we lived and saw our car. It seemed odd to me that he would ask this in my dream. In fact, I was wondering how he even knew what my car looked like.

He stared awkwardly at me for a moment and then said, "Guess I better get this sweeping done because today is wax day for these floors. It is always a chore to keep this darn place looking nice." He then took his eyes off me and slowly began pushing his large dust mop.

The dream immediately changed venues, and I saw a powerplant that appeared to be under construction. I was walking from the outside into what looked like the boiler room. I saw MPS – 89 pulverizers. These were the same pulverizers we have at LRS, but in my dream each pulverizer had a large primary air fan connected to it. I had never seen this arrangement before.

I then slowly turned and looked at the bottom ash hoppers under the boiler. They were very odd-looking. The hoppers had a large, ascending, rectangular chute at a 45° angle and bottom ash slowly dropped off the top of the chute. I then walked outside the plant. I saw dusty plant grounds from the blowing wind as the door opened. Off in the distance, I saw the cooling tower. I had a distinct feeling of peace and intrigue combined. It just felt good there. I had no idea why it felt good. I then awakened.

I gathered my thoughts and realized this dream appeared to have the same format as the previous ones which were obviously from the Lord. I thought about the plant but didn't have a clue where it was. I drifted back to sleep. That morning, I awakened again with the same feeling of peace and intrigue. I wasn't sure what to think.

I had a light breakfast and headed for the plant. I arrived in the parking lot and walked into the plant via the administration building. This was my standard way of going to the control room and Shift office, so I wasn't doing anything different. As soon as I passed through the vestibule and into the admin I turned left to go out to the plant. Tom Sawyer, the admin building janitor was there with a large dust mop. My heart jumped into my throat.

"Hi!" he said boisterously in his high-pitched, grating voice. "Do you live in a white and black house on Elm Street?" *EXACTLY* like I saw in the dream; he was leaning against the handle of his large dust mop and had his head cocked to one side.

"Yes... I do.... *Why do you ask?*" I answered haltingly because I was blown away by the clarity of the dream to the real situation.

"I was just wondering. It looked like your car in the driveway the other day." Just like in the dream, he stared at me for a moment and continued. "Guess I better get this psweeping done because today is the wax day for these floors. It is always a chore to keep this darn place looking nice."

I was shocked but not fully surprised. This was, word for word, what I saw and heard in the dream.

"I hope you have a nice day!" I replied as he started pushing the dust mop.

He stopped and turned his head back towards me. "Yup, these darn floors ain't gonna clean themselves, that's for sure!" He snorfed a chuckle and resumed pushing the dust mop.

I went on to the Shift Supervisor's office and did shift turnover. I was oddly curious because I knew that I saw another plant and I was intrigued by it.

That evening during dinner I decided to bait Vangie about possibly leaving Wheatland. "So, if I had a chance to go to another new power plant, I was wondering if you would consider leaving Wheatland?" I was trying not to sound cryptic, but I knew it came off this way.

"Why?" She looked at me suspiciously. "Do you have a plant you think you want to go to?"

"I just had an odd dream last night. In the dream I saw another plant." I never told her the details of the Disneyworld dream other than telling her I had it. She was aware of the Gerry Shiftler dream and what happened to him.

"Where was it?" she asked while still looking at me suspiciously.

"I don't know. It just seemed like the right place to me in the dream, but I am not certain."

"Talk to me when you know something definitive." She seemed a bit irritated. This was not uncommon when discussing something like this. Vangie saw everything as being black or white. There were seldom any gray areas in her thinking. Me coming to her with a cryptic question about something I saw in a dream would not bait her into a conversation.

I knew many the plants being constructed at the time. There was the Valmy Plant in Nevada, White Bluff and Independence in Arkansas, Gibbons Creek in Texas, Holcomb Station in Kansas, Rawhide Plant in Colorado, Craig Plant in Colorado, Intermountain Power Project in Utah, and even Basin Electric was starting on the Antelope Valley Station in North Dakota.

On my next day off I called around and got the phone number of Platte River Power Authority, the company building the Rawhide Plant near Fort Collins. We could see the early construction activities west of I-25 when we traveled to Fort Collins. My attempts to call yielded little. They had not even selected a Plant Manager yet.

I was able to call the Intermountain Power Project in Delta, Utah. It was a HUGE project owned primarily by the Los Angeles Department of Water and Power. They were building two 850 MW coal units that would transmit all the power onto a D.C. (Direct Current) line to California. However, they were not ready to hire Shift Supervisors because they were too early in construction. They took my name and said they would contact me when they were ready to accept resumes'.

I then looked in the employment section of Power Engineering© Magazine and found a number for Sunflower Electric, the company building the Holcomb Station in Kansas.

I called the number and was transferred to Bill Elfman. He was the Operations Manager at the plant.

"This is Bill Elfman. Who am I speaking with?" The voice at the end of the line seemed strained or maybe very bored.

"Mark Gregg. I am an Assistant Shift Supervisor at Laramie River Station in Wheatland, Wyoming, and I saw you might be in the process of staffing a new coal-fired plant."

"Indeed, we are. In fact, we are interviewing for Shift Supervisors right now."

"If it is not too late, could I send you my resume'?" I then added, "I might be interested in interviewing for a Shift Supervisor's job." I felt compelled to get my resume' to him.

"It is not too late." He replied bluntly. "We have several interviews scheduled and have made one offer so far. However, I wouldn't waste any time sending your resume." He paused. "Could you FAX it to me?"

"I can do that. Can you give me your FAX number?" He shuffled some papers and then read me his FAX number.

"I don't actually have a resume' typed up yet but I will do so immediately and get it to you." I felt embarrassed telling him this.

"Not a problem. Just get it FAXED to me and if you are what we are looking for, I will give you a callback."

The next night I finished shift turnover and took care of some issues with the plant and the scrubber. I was hoping it would be a quiet night because I wanted to get the resume' typed. It took until about 0400 in the morning to break free long enough to go into the admin area and use an IBM© Selectric© typewriter. They were self-correcting... *Truly a Godsend for a non-typist like me.*

When I finally finished the frustrating odyssey of typing the two-page document I had just enough time to FAX it to Bill Elfman at Sunflower Electric before shift turnover. I am glad I FAXED it so he couldn't see that it had several layers of correction fluid on every other word. I garnered a lot more respect for the secretaries that night as I painstakingly pecked out my resume'.

I arrived back home and was interrupted in my shower by Vangie saying a man from Sunflower Electric named Bill Elfman was on the phone. I told her I would call him right back. I quickly finished my shower and went straight to the phone, dialing the number he gave Vangie.

He immediately answered the call. "Bill Elfman Speaking." His voice had more of an air of urgency today.

"Bill, this is Mark Gregg. I was in the shower when you called a bit ago."

"I know. That is what your wife said." He chuckled. "I am guessing you did your resume on a typewriter at the plant during the graveyard shift and then FAXED it from there." He paused and chuckled again. "Am I right?" I immediately felt my face flushing.

"Umm... Yes, you would be correct." I decided honesty was obviously the best policy.

"Frankly, I am glad you didn't have resumes' already finished. It tells me that you are not just a job hopper."

"Oh, no, sir, I am not. We just finished starting the three 600-megawatt units here at LRS and I would honestly like to start another one and frankly, would not mind getting out of Wyoming." I drew a quick breath. "Wheatland is a one-horse town, and I noticed on a map that Garden City appears to be a larger town." I was trying to sound as professional as possible.

"Are you married?"

"Yes sir, I am. We have two little girls. One is almost six, and the other is almost three."

"How does your wife feel about moving?" It was obvious I was being interviewed. This was okay because I didn't have time to obsess about it. I was just rolling with the punches.

"She is fine with it. She is no more enamored with Wheatland than I am."

"Hmmm." He mumbled something, but I didn't catch what it was. He then cleared his throat and continued. "Can you tell me about the Power Load Unbalance circuit on your G.E. turbines?"

I explained in precise detail what the PLU circuit was, why it is needed, and how it worked.

"Okay. Good. Can you tell me what the optimum primary air velocity is on an MPS pulverizer?"

"3500 feet per minute." I was somewhat guessing on this one.

"Again, Good. When can you fly to the Holcomb Plant for a formal interview?"

I was surprised at how fast this was going. I wanted to call in sick for some of my graveyard shifts but didn't want to tip my hand that I HATED shift work. "I can probably come during my long change. I have six-night shifts to finish, and I will then have my long change free. I can come, then."

"Excellent! I will have Gloria Grimes, our human resource girl, phone you early next week and work out the travel details." He seemed upbeat. "We encourage you to bring your wife to Garden City. While you will get a paid house-hunting trip if we offer you a position, we would also like the wives to come and see the area."

"That is great to hear. I am not sure we have anyone to watch the kids, but if we can find someone, I am certain she would enjoy coming with me."

"Excellent, I look forward to meeting you, Mark."

"Same here. I am excited about seeing the plant also."

We finished and hung up the phone.

Vangie wanted to accompany me so we called Marie Marquette to see if she and Milton would consider watching the kids. Marie was gracious and agreed to help us. Without talking to Gloria, Sunflower's human resources person, I figured that it would be a very quick trip out and back. Marie would only have to watch the kids for two days and one night.

Monday rolled around and Gloria called not long after I arrived home from the graveyard shift that morning. Garden City is on central time, and Wheatland is on Mountain Time, so it worked out well. Gloria sounded young and petite and was very hospitable with the travel arrangements. I made it clear that we wanted in and out as quickly as possible.

We had to fly from Denver to Garden City, which meant driving to Denver. They were paying us IRS guidelines for mileage. Gloria went on to explain how they would pay all moving expenses, including packing/unpacking, and give us an all-expense paid house hunting trip along with a $2,000.00 bonus upon arrival if I were hired. In 1982, $2,000.00 was a substantial amount of money. It excited me and increased my anxiety about the interview.

Sunflower Electric Cooperative was headquartered in Hays, Kansas. It was formed in 1957 by several smaller cooperatives that saw the need for a larger company that could serve them with dependable power sources. Initially, Sunflower was primarily a wire company, meaning they handled the transmission and distribution system for their rural customers and bought power off the grid. They had a few small, gas-fired generating stations and they were now building a large coal-fired plant to self-supply all the member cooperatives.

Wednesday morning, I arrived home from work and crawled into bed. Vangie said she would take the kids to Milt and Marie's and be ready to leave when I awakened at about

11

noon. As always, she was ultra-prepared and ready to go. All I had to do was get some rest and she took care of everything else.

The drive to Denver was good, but the flight to Garden City was on a Fairchild Metroliner. If I had to pick one of the most miserable small commuter planes ever built, the Metroliner would be it. It was like sitting in a deafening and claustrophobic stovepipe. It seated 19 people with 'intimate' seating (this was the description used in their seat-pocket information), and there was no separation between the pilot and the passengers. It had gangly long landing gear and looked like a water bug out of water when it was taxiing.

The flight to Garden City left this hapless little turboprop at the mercy of the unforgiving atmospheric whims of the Great Plains. We were up, down, jostled, and bumped the entire flight. The landing in Garden City was terrifying. The crosswind was bad enough that it felt like we were landing sideways, only to have our bodies snapped forward when the wheels assaulted the runway and corrected for the crosswind. Luckily, the pilot and copilot looked to be in their late teens or early twenties, so they obviously had tons of hours flying. In fairness, they seemed to do a good job... *Any landing you walk away from is a good landing, right?*

Gloria Grimes reserved us a rental car at the Garden City airport. It was already dark by the time we retrieved our luggage and secured the rental car. We looked around Garden City a bit before checking into the Hilton Hotel. Garden City was substantially larger than Wheatland but slightly smaller than Cheyenne, Wyoming.

12

Garden City Community College was established there in the early 1900's. It was a modern, sizable community college. The aging downtown area was still in decent shape, and we were fascinated by the original cobblestone streets in the center of town. They had a large zoo, and some nice parks. After looking around town, we had an enjoyable dinner at the Hilton that evening and went to bed.

My interview was with Curt Brunz, the Plant Manager, Bill Elfman, the Operations Superintendent, and Brad Schultz, the Operations Supervisor. Curt was trim, handsome, and in his late 40's. Bill was burly, sloppy, and was probably pushing 55 or so years old. Brad appeared to be about my age. He was tall, gaunt, pale-skinned, and blonde. He was _never_ without a cigarette in his hand.

Brad reminded me of a stereotypical used car salesman. Fast-talking, always confident of what he was spouting, and nervous... Eternally nervous. The continuous, rapid, and deep draws on his cigarette seemed to provide an elusive and momentary calm to get him through to the next draw.

It was obvious during the interview that Brad and Curt were close buddies. They both came from the Coal Creek facility in Washburn, North Dakota. It is two 550 MW lignite (brown coal) fired, mine-mouth units in North Dakota. Because Coal Creek Plant was burning some of the lowest quality fuel in the country, they had the distinction of physically being the largest boilers in the world and yet, they were only 550 MW each. Heck, Curt and Brad weren't just buddies, they could have been husband and wife. They finished each other's sentences.

Their closeness wasn't lost on Bill Elfman. He had a saggy but very demonstrative face that continuously flashed small grimaces as Curt and Brad reminisced about the good old days at Coal Creek. They had only been at Sunflower for a month. *The good old days were not that old.* It turned out that Curt was a Shift Supervisor at Coal Creek, and Brad was his Control Room Operator. Moving directly from a Shift Supervisor to Plant Manager is a big jump that rarely happens.

During the interview they told me about the small town of Holcomb, which is about five miles from the plant. This is where the heinous mass-murder of the Clutter family occurred in 1959. Truman Capote wrote his book about the Clutter family titled, *"In Cold Blood"* in 1966. It became a best seller in the non-fiction category.

I found it interesting that this was brought up in the interview. If you are truly recruiting the best people to operate your plant, I would think you would choose a more positive image of the area than highlighting a mass murder where a family was slaughtered in cold blood in their own home with a shotgun at close range.

Bill was quirky and hard to read. His background was primarily nuclear with his career starting at the Zuni Street station for Public Service Co. of Colorado. This was an old, *real old*, gas-fired plant in downtown Denver that, in recent years had been relegated to central heating duties for the downtown area. Bill left Zuni and went to the now defunct Fort Saint Vrain experimental gas-cooled reactor plant and spent many years there working on his Registered Professional Engineer License while waiting for something to happen at the plant. I learned a little about this plant from reading Power Engineering magazine.

Frankly, Bill was older and very smart but had *little practical operating experience*. Zuni was a small gas-fired boiler plant, and the nuke plant did not run more than a few hundred hours during its entire existence. Bill was a curmudgeon and an egghead that had less real-world coal-fired plant operating experience than I did, and I certainly did not have a lot.

The interview was a cinch. The technical questions were not difficult and their seemingly most important question, "Why did I want to move?" was easy to explain. Wheatland sucked; Garden City appeared to be much nicer.

They pointed out that the largest beef packing plant in the world was being built a few miles from the Holcomb plant and that Garden City often smelled of the massive cattle fattening facilities (feed lots) that surrounded it in every direction. Indeed, Vangie and I had already experienced the malodorous cacophony in the evening breezes at the Hilton Inn. It reduced the allure of Garden City but didn't eliminate it.

We finished the interview, and they introduced me to Bob Ellington. He was the new Plant Engineer. He came from the Gibson Plant in Indiana. It was 5, 600 MW units, and he was very proud of it. It was all he could talk about every time you were around him.

After meeting Bob Ellington, the interview concluded with a walk-through of the partially completed facility. As soon as we walked into the plant my previous dream *RACED* into focus. We walked past the condensate polishers and over to the immense MPS–89 coal pulverizers. I instantly did a double take. They were *EXACTLY* what I saw in the dream. Each pulverizer was directly fed by a large primary air fan. I

15

had never seen this before other than in my dream that fateful night a month or so back.

As I stared at the pulverizer/PA fan set-up, Bill nudged me.

"Take a look at this," he said, slowly pointing behind the primary air fans.

I turned and looked at the bottom ash hoppers under the boiler. It was the craziest thing I had ever seen. The hoppers had a huge, ascending, rectangular chute at a 45° angle. It was exactly what I saw in the dream! It was not a reasonable facsimile; it was precisely what I saw in the dream other than in the dream it had ash dropping off the incline conveyor.

"This is the first water-cooled, incline drag chain ash conveyor in the United States!" Bill exclaimed as he pointed toward the large, inclined chute. "We are the first plant in North America to install this type of drag chain. It was designed and fabricated in Germany." We walked under it and then climbed the steps on the side of the massive chain and bar assembly.

As he talked, I was lost in awe of the fact that I saw something in my dream that I didn't know existed and had never seen before. How can this be? I had never seen pulverizers directly connected to individual primary air fans. LRS had two common primary air fans that used ductwork to supply the individual MPS pulverizers. Yet, I clearly saw these pulverizers and this specific bottom ash system in my dream. This cannot be possible. My mind cannot make something up that I didn't know existed, *right*?

We walked out of the east door of the plant, and déjà vu hit me square in the face again. I saw the dusty plant grounds from the blowing wind. Off in the distance I saw the cooling tower. I had a combined feeling of peace and intrigue. The mind-numbing reality that I had already lived these past several minutes a month earlier in my dream was not lost on me.

I finished the interview with enough time for Vangie and I to drive around Garden City again, this time in the daylight. We made it a point to drive by the largest free municipal swimming pool in the United States. This was one of Garden City's claim to fame. We found out later that it was advertised on road signs that come in and out of town on all major roads for over 50 miles. It was indeed, a very large pool, and the fact that it was free to the public was interesting.

Overall, Garden City seemed like a decent place. They even had a relatively large zoo for a small town. If there was a negative it was the smell of the feed lots. Depending on where you were and the direction of the wind, the smell would activate your gag reflexes. Other than this, it seemed like a whole lot nicer place than Wheatland.

The trip back to Denver on the Metroliner was as noisy and unsettling as the trip into Garden City. However, we were able to land, get our luggage, ride the shuttle to the parking lot, and drive back to Wheatland without incident. We crawled into bed at about 1:00 in the morning.

The three-hour drive from Stapleton Airport to Wheatland was consumed by discussions on them possibly making a good offer. Vangie coveted Milt and Marie's friendship and liked the fact that her sister, Bernadette, was now living in

17

Wheatland. I had not even considered either of these things when I agreed to interview at the Holcomb Station.

A few years prior to us moving to Wheatland, Vangie's younger sister Bernadette married an older man named Mike Rood. She was a rebellious 16-year-old girl; he was about 30 when they married. He had already been married to another girl much younger than him prior to Bernadette, but she apparently wised up and divorced him.

My only interaction with Mike was when Vangie and I traveled back to Montrose to attend their wedding. Vangie's oldest sister, Gloria and her husband, Patrick were there. Pat and I decided to go to the A&W Root Beer stand and get a gallon of root beer. This was something I had done many times when we still lived in Montrose. It was kind of a 'thing' for me. I loved the cloyingly sweet root beer, and it was always fun to get a gallon and some ice cream and make everyone root beer floats. Silly but enjoyable.

Patrick, Mike and I went to the A&W root beer stand and gave the carhop our order for a gallon of A&W's ultra-sweet elixir. The carhop just happened to be a young, cute girl. Mike immediately started hitting on her. Pat and I could not believe it. He was marrying the sister of our wives the very next day and was overtly flirting with the waitress/carhop like he was 15 years younger and unattached.

Pat asked him why he was doing this. He just laughed and said, "it never hurts to window shop. Besides, it's fun!" Pat and I were both disgusted. Bernadette was probably not prepared to hear anything negative about her husband-to-be on her wedding eve.

Bernadette became pregnant not long after marrying Mike and had a beautiful baby girl named Desiree'. After a couple of years of unfaithfulness and abuse from Mike, Bernadette divorced him. Nick Moore, my racing buddy and High School friend then began dating Bernadette.

Nick had never been married and Bernadette was still hurting from her horrible experience with Mike Rood, so they just cohabitated. They were living in Grand Junction, Colorado at the time and Nick was a cable television installer. He was working long hours for little pay, and they were barely making a living.

I talked to Nick about putting in an application at the plant. He gladly did so, and I went to Bert on Nick's behalf and gave a grand sales pitch about how good of an employee he would be. Truth is, I had no idea how good of an employee he would be. I just knew that he needed a decent job to support himself, Bernadette, and Desiree'.

It worked… Basin Electric hired him as an entry-level operator, and they moved to Wheatland. Not long after arriving, they tied the knot in a small wedding. It turned out that Bernadette was pregnant with their son Jesse at the time. Ultimately, everything worked out because they are still together to this day and still living in Wheatland. Nick was an excellent operator for many years before retiring from the plant.

Up to this point we moved as the job situation dictated. Vangie never really questioned the need to change jobs and move. I never considered the fact that we had family in Wheatland now. I am not just talking about Nick and Bernadette but about Milt and Marie. I was as close to Milt as

I was to my own brothers. Moving had now morphed into something that required deep, soulful decision-making. We hadn't dealt with this prior to now, and it appeared it was going to be difficult.

For the first time ever, I was questioning making a move. The conflict was greater than Vangie knew because I could not escape the reality of seeing the plant in the dream in the detail that I saw it. *This had to mean something.*

CHAPTER 2
THE MOVE TO GARDEN CITY, KANSAS

There was very little wait before Sunflower Electric made an offer. It came that next Monday morning. I had just slid under a car I was working on for someone at the plant when Vangie stuck her head out the garage door. "Mark, Bill Elfman is on the phone. Should I tell him you will call him back?"

"No!" I exclaimed. "I will come and talk to him. Let me wipe my hands off." I slid out from under the car, wiped a layer of grease off my hands, rushing inside. I was breathing hard due to the shot of adrenaline hitting me when she told me Bill Elfman was on the phone.

"This is Mark," I said, trying not to sound out of breath.

"Mark, this is Bill Elfman at the Holcomb Plant. Do you have a few minutes?"

"Certainly." I drew a quick breath. "I want to thank you for the plant tour and the hospitality Sunflower Electric provided during the interview last week. I was going to call and thank you today, but you beat me to the punch!"

"No problem." He cleared his throat. "I am calling to offer you the position of Shift Supervisor at the Holcomb Station. I think Gloria Grimes has explained our benefits to you, and you already know about the $2,000.00 bonus for coming on board." He stopped, cleared his throat again, and then continued. "We will provide a house hunting trip and will pay a moving company to pack and move all of your household goods." I started to respond, but he cut me off. "We are offering you a $26,500.00 per year salary. I know you are making more than this now, but the salary will obviously increase once the unit is running."

I was surprised that the offer was this low. I was making almost $5,000 a year more at Basin Electric. I started to speak a second time, but he jumped in again.

"You will be a full Shift Supervisor, not an Assistant, and will get to help interview and hire your own crew members." I waited to see if he was going to keep talking this time before saying anything.

"I am definitely making more than that now… Is there negotiation room?" I kept my voice upbeat because I didn't want to offend or rub him the wrong way.

"No, there isn't. This is the maximum we can offer any Shift Supervisor at this stage. At least you will know that the other four Shift Supervisors are not making more than you." His voice sounded strained as he answered. He knew this was a low-ball offer. I understood I would have to take a pay cut. It was just like leaving Four Corners for LRS. However, I was disappointed at how much of a pay cut it was.

"I will tentatively say yes to your offer. However, I need to discuss this with Vangie and get back to you."

"No problem. You talk to your wife and get back to me at your earliest convenience. In the meantime, I will make sure Gloria sends you the offer in writing." He seemed relieved. I am certain he was expecting a hard "NO" from me. I figured he had already experienced rejections from other applicants. It was interesting that they could spend over a billion dollars to build a new plant but not try to be more competitive with salaries.

I hung up the phone and turned to Vangie. "They offered me the Shift Supervisor position."

"Did he tell you how much you would be making?" As always, she was very pointed in her response.

"$26,500.00 a year salary."

"Aren't you making a lot more than that now?" she said with a grimace on her face.

"About $5,000.00 more."

She stared at me a moment and with no emotion before asking, "what are you going to do?"

I countered with, "What do you think we should do?"

She turned defensive. "You have to make this decision, not me."

"I know it is my decision... I just need to know what you want to do."

Her demeanor immediately turned stern, "Leave me out of this. Just make your decision and stick with it."

"You have a say in this!" I exclaimed, raising my voice. "Tell me if YOU want to move."

"Mark, you are going to do what you want to do, so just make your decision and tell me what it is." I could tell she was getting angry. I was now getting irritated at her because it seemed she inferred I was uninterested in her opinion.

"All I am asking is…" I paused to control my voice so as not to be combative. "Do you, or do you not want to move to Garden City?"

She gave me her (dreaded) angry eyes. "Look, you already told him you were going to take the job. Why are you playing this game with me?" I then realized she had heard my conversation with Bill and knew I told him I was tentatively accepting the job.

"All I did was buy time so we can talk about this together and decide if we want to move there." I lowered my voice and tried to sound more consoling. "I have learned to never slam the door on anything until it is the right time."

"You make your decision and let me know. I have to check on the kids." She turned and walked back towards the bedrooms. I was pissed. I just wanted to know what she thought. I wasn't trying to ram anything down her throat.

I went back outside and continued working on the car in our garage while my temper cooled. I decided the cut in pay was substantial enough that we would have to sell the Saab. I had a thing for Saab automobiles in those days. To me, they were exotic, and I liked the way the turbo-charged engines ran. I bought and sold a couple of the turbo-charged versions. I had to buy and sell them because we really couldn't afford to keep the more expensive turbo models.

We still owned two Saabs. One was a 1978 Saab 99. It was a 'work car' that I bought cheaply in Denver. It had a gazillion miles on it but ran perfectly. Our 1979 Saab 900 was a GLE four-door. I also bought it in Denver and paid way too much. It was not in the best of shape for being only two years old, plus it was an ugly brown color. It's not the most popular color for a car like this. The monthly payment was high on it. Truth be known, I should have never purchased it in the first place. I knew this car would have to go away if we moved to Garden City.

After cooling down I decided to tackle the subject of moving again with Vangie. I navigated a slightly different route this time. She was playing with the kids when I came back into the house.

"Whoa, you smell like gasoline!" she exclaimed as I walked into the front room.

"Sorry!" I said quickly. "Do you think it would be a good idea to fly back to Garden City for a house-hunting trip to see if we can even afford a decent house?"

"Who will watch the kids?" I could see this was going to be a bit more difficult than I thought.

"I don't know. Maybe Milt and Marie again?"

"You need to figure out the details and then make the decision. A house hunting trip sounds too long to leave the kids with Milt and Marie again.

"Fine, but would you go with me?"

"Not if you can't figure out what you are doing with the kids."

I wasn't pleased because she was making it difficult. However, I knew I should accept what she said for now. I never considered that she was just being thoughtful and considerate. A house-hunting trip would be far too long to leave the kids with Milt and Marie.

The next few days at LRS I could not get my mind away from the Holcomb Station. The images of the dream matching the plant and the general feeling of excitement while at the plant haunted me. I felt like we should be there.

I decided that we would make a trip to Montrose and leave the girls with Vangie's parents. We would then travel back to Denver, catch the flight to Garden City, and then do the reverse after the house-hunting trip. This would be a major undertaking. I wasn't sure how Vangie would handle it.

I called Vangie's parents and discussed the potential babysitting duties with them. They were awesome people and immediately came up with a much better idea. They would come to Wheatland and watch the kids at our house. This would allow them to see all three of their grandkids... Brandi, Brittanie, and Bernadette's daughter, Desiree'... Woo Hoo! *This could not have worked out any better.*

Vangie was amenable to this and seemed fine with going on the house-hunting trip. This pleased me. I called Bill Elfman and told him I would do the house-hunting trip.

Arranging vacation for my next graveyard shift was a bit more challenging than I thought due to the "short notice" but Bert relinquished and gave me the time off. Whew! A lot had to come together in a short period of time for this house-hunting trip to happen.

The dayshift run went particularly fast as we had many plant issues at LRS. On one of the days, we went black-plant (lost all incoming station service) on unit − 2 due to some relay work being done in the switchyard. I enjoyed the thrill of these events.

During my final day shift, Alex and Cordie arrived bearing gifts for the children and a bigger gift for us… *The gift of babysitting*! We spent an afternoon and evening with them leaving on the house-hunting trip the next morning. The Metroliner nightmare from Stapleton to Garden City did not disappoint! Those nasty little aircraft were obnoxious, noisy pieces of crap.

Gloria made it clear we could pick any realtor we wanted in Garden City so long as it was Neil Mecklenburg. Seriously, she said we could use anyone but she "highly recommended" Neil. We took her advice. We figured she had a reason for recommending him and she was paying the entire bill for the house-hunting trip, so we flowed with it.

Neil was a bit of a curmudgeon. However, he had a dry wit and was about as laid-back as anyone I ever met. Sometimes, I wasn't sure if he was even breathing. Fortunately, despite his low-key demeanor, he knew the real estate market in Garden City quite well.

We never let the grass grow under our feet. We went through many neighborhoods, old and new, to get a feel for what the town was like and where real estate was available. The problem was, and it was a HUGE problem, the prevailing mortgage interest rates. They were almost 15%. This made home ownership extremely difficult.

We were able to buy our home in Wheatland with an amazing 7% interest rate thanks to the Wyoming Community Development Fund (WCDF). Unfortunately, there appeared to be nothing like this in Garden City. The only respite for high interest rates was ARMs, or Adjustable-Rate Mortgages.

As the name implies, the ARM mortgage rate was adjustable and allowed you to get into a house at a lower rate, but it was subject to increase in a short period of time and required frequent refinancing. I did not like this approach at all. However, it was the only way we could even look at a house with any chance of being able to afford it. Even with the adjustable-rate mortgage, the payment was quite high due to the excessive interest rate.

It didn't take us long to get discouraged. The houses in our price range were older, smaller homes. If we wanted to be in a newer section of town, it narrowed down to the Indian Hills subdivision. This was a relatively new subdivision on the east side of town. Most of the homes were very small with small yards. Most homes in Garden City had basements. I don't know if it was because of the tornado risk or the low water table. I beleive it was a combination of both.

We found a home at 2108 Arapaho Drive in Indian Hills that we somewhat liked. It was about 7 years old and 960 Sq Feet but had a full basement that was nicely finished. There was nothing fancy about the house, but it was in good shape. It had a one-car attached garage. Without a large amount of money as a down payment, the house payment was going to be substantially higher than the house payment we were currently paying in Wheatland. This house was certainly not any nicer than the house in Wheatland and had a smaller yard. This discouraged both of us.

Reality finally abounded. We probably couldn't make the move due to being unable to afford a decent house. We decided to simply see what else was available in Garden City regardless of price. What the heck? We were already there and had nothing else to do.

Neil taxied us all over town, usually showing us homes that we could not possibly consider due to their price. The more we saw, the more convinced I was that we couldn't move. This was right up until we were heading west on Mary Street, a primary thoroughfare through Garden City.

There was nothing about this moment that would have prompted what happened. I clearly remember being discouraged and thinking ahead about finishing this lame trip and going back home to Wheatland.

As we traveled down Mary Street, I clearly, unquestionably heard the following words, *"IT CANNOT BE STOPPED NOW."* That was it; there was nothing else. It snapped me instantly out of my wandering thoughts and prompted my heartbeat to double.

These words did not come from Neil or Vangie. I looked over at Neil who was driving with his usual relaxed, distant look, and then back at Vangie, who chose to sit in the back seat. When I looked back at her she just gave me a minimal 'courtesy smile' that I am certain would have been the same if I hadn't heard what I knew I just heard.

To this day and this moment, I know I heard this. It was clear and concise and did not come from my brain because it was the farthest thing from my brain at that time. I am certain that anyone reading this will probably explain it away in some form or fashion. Don't. It was real, and I will testify to this on my deathbed. I clearly heard, *"IT CANNOT BE STOPPED NOW."*

The remainder of the house-hunting trip was a blur. Even if we were serious about buying a house in Garden City, we would still have to sell our home in Wheatland. Therefore, Vangie and I just enjoyed the 'visit' to Garden City and returned to Wheatland.

Despite the words I heard on Mary Street during the house hunting trip, I called Bill Elfman to tell him we could not possibly move to Garden City due to home prices, interest rates, and not being able to afford a decent home. He seemed extremely disappointed but said he understood. Apparently, this was somewhat of a theme. He indicated several others did this same thing after the house-hunting trip.

Vangie and I discussed the move and we both agreed that there was no way I could take the job at Holcomb Station because of our current financial situation, the $5,000.00 a year cut in pay, and the cost of housing due to high mortgage interest costs. The payment for even a cheap house was out of reach for us because we did not have an adequate amount of money to use as a down payment. I was disappointed and confused. However, *the initial dream leading us to Garden City and the voice on Mary Street still haunted me.*

That evening, I prayed a very simple prayer. I said, "Lord, if it was You that said it cannot be stopped now, then You must have a plan. We must sell the Saab and sell this house for enough money to allow us to buy something in Garden City." That was it. Nothing huge, no travail, just a simple prayer.

I went back to work on my first afternoon shift, extremely grateful that I did not have to do the graveyard shifts. With all my vacation time now spent, I would have to knuckle down and do the graveyard shifts for quite some time before I built up enough vacation to miss some more.

Even though I turned down the job at Holcomb Station, I called the Casper newspaper and put in a 3-day advertisement for the Saab. I wanted to eliminate its high monthly payment and was tired of the car. I tired easily of cars. *It seems wanting is always better than having.*

Frankly, I wasn't holding a lot of promise to sell it because Saab's hadn't really caught on yet in Wyoming, or any place else for that matter. The turbocharged versions were a little more popular, but the four-door 900 GLE was going to be a definite *hard sell*.

The next day, a Wednesday, I went to work and ran into Tom Sawyer in the admin building. He was behind his broom. As with the previous time we talked, the odd little man struck up a conversation with me.

"Mark, does your house on Elm Street have a WCDF funded mortgage?" Part of me wanted to tell him that it was none of his business. However, he seemed sincere enough.

"Yes, it does, why?" I asked curiously.

"Just wondering." His screechy voice and run-on sentences were difficult to listen to. "If you ever want to sell it let me know cuz I would like to buy a house like yours with a low-interest loan that is assumable like the WCDF loans cuz the payment is something I can probably afford cuz I want to move my Mom and me there." He then gave me a goofy-looking grin. He was somewhat of a spectacle, as round as he was tall and tightly curled, black hair with that odd case of pattern baldness.

"Believe it or not, I actually might be interested in selling it." I said haltingly. "I will let you know if this is the case or not." I looked directly at him. "You honestly think you are interested?"

"Oh, yes I am, yes I am!" He wheezed. "The low-interest money is not available any longer so I will have to assume an existing loan like yours." He smiled broadly. "I have been livin' with my Mom and savin money for a long time now." He grinned and opened his eyes oddly wide.

"That's great!" I said quickly. "I have to get upstairs for shift change, but I will let you know."

"Yup, these floors ain't goin' to clean themselves..." He mumbled and started sweeping again as I went to the Shift Supervisor's office.

I finished shift turnover and was tending to some problems in the scrubber when Vangie called the plant looking for me. This was very rare. When the control room paged me and said she was on the phone, I was concerned because I figured something happened to one of the kids. I rushed to the control room and called her back immediately.

"Is everything okay?" I asked quickly as she answered the phone.

"Yes, everything is fine. I just got a call from a guy named Jerry McCloskey. He said he was in Cheyenne and was heading back to Casper. He wanted to know if he could come by and see the Saab. She paused. "He just gave me a phone number and said to call him back."

"Wow, that was quick. The ad would have just hit the paper today."

"Here is his number, you can call him back." She gave me his phone number, and I called him after we hung up.

Sure enough, he saw the advertisement for the Saab in the Casper newspaper and wanted to drop by that evening on his way from Cheyenne to Casper. I told him it wasn't a problem and if he could pinpoint approximately when he would arrive, I would slip out of the plant and come to the house (if nothing major was happening at the plant).

He arrived at about 8:00 PM. It was a dark evening. A layer of clouds obscured any moonlight. He was alone and probably in his mid-50's. He didn't say much as he walked around the car. He asked to drive it, so I let him take it for a spin. He returned about 5 minutes later and simply said, "I will take it."

I was completely shocked. I don't believe I ever sold a car (and I sold plenty of them) that someone didn't try and offer less or haggle. Nope. He did none of this. There was no haggling whatsoever. He just said he wanted the car. He wrote me a check and said he would be back the next afternoon with his wife to pick it up. I told him I would have to pay it off at the bank to get the title but would do so in the morning. He was satisfied with this and left.

It was a completely surreal moment. Not only did he not try to haggle about the price, but he was also a man of few words. He simply bought the car and left. Oddly, the 3–day ad in the Casper paper never produced another call. *None.* Had he not purchased it, it would not have sold.

I looked at Vangie as he drove out of the cul-de-sac and said, "I hope you are okay with moving to Garden City."

"Why?" she asked curiously. "You already told them we weren't coming. Why would you say this now?"

I looked at her intensely and said, "The Saab sold instantly, and Tom Sawyer, the admin building janitor, stopped me in the hall and asked if we wanted to sell our house."

"Why would he do that? Are you telling people it is for sale?" I wasn't sure if she was angry or just intensely curious.

"No. He just stopped me in the hall and asked if we had a WCDF loan. I told him we did, and he said he wanted to buy the house if we were going to sell it. Apparently he needs the low-interest loan to afford the payments."

"You mean, like us?" She answered very pointedly.

Her demeanor was snarky, but I don't think she was trying to be obnoxious. Maybe I'm wrong. Sometimes I couldn't tell.

"Probably so." I gave her a quick hug. "I have to get back to the plant. If I am not there and something happens, I would be in big trouble."

The next morning, I went down to Haeberle Realty. We used this real estate company to buy our house and they handled the mortgage through the WCDF. As I understood it previously, the loan was fully assumable so long as the buyer met all the guidelines we originally met.

I told Steve, the real estate agent, that Tom Sawyer might be in to talk to him and asked if he would be willing to handle the sale and get him qualified for the WCDF loan assumption. He was more than happy to do so.

I asked Steve what the house was currently worth. We only lived there for two years but we did put in the yard, and I recently did some framing in the basement. I purchased and carried in a ton of sheetrock and lumber but had barely begun the basement framing process. Steve gave me his best guess of its value and it appeared we had made about $3,500.00 on the house by living in it for two years and expending the labor to put in a modest yard. I told him to use this number when talking with Tom.

I left for work early the next day and found Tom in the Admin building. I told him about Haeberle Realty and that I wanted to sell our house. When I told him the price, he seemed overjoyed… He was almost childishly happy, assuring me he would take off work the next morning and start the purchase process.

Could it really be this easy? It didn't make sense that the car and the house would simply go away this fast. I called Neil Mecklenburg and asked him if the house at 2108 Arapaho was still on the market. He said it was. I then immediately called Bill Elfman and asked if my position was still open. He assured me it was and added that he would be happy to have me there.

I called Neil Mecklenburg right back about the house on Arapaho Street. We decided to put in a very low offer contingent upon the sale of our house to Tom Sawyer and our ability to secure a new loan for the Arapaho house. That night, after getting off work, I had to mail an earnest money check to Neil so he could validate the offer.

We wouldn't have had the money to do this if the Saab hadn't sold because we made about $350.00 on it. *Oddly, this was the amount that Neil required as earnest money for the Arapaho offer.* I was still in complete disbelief over the Saab selling so quickly for the asking price.

I started my day shifts the next week, but not before hearing from Neil. He sounded excited and exclaimed that they took our offer without countering. The house on Arapaho was now ours for the price we offered contingent upon Tom consummating the sale of our house and us qualifying for a loan on the new house.

Again, could it really be this easy? My head was spinning. How could these things fall into place so quickly? On my second dayshift, Steve Haeberle called me and said that Tom Sawyer was, "good as gold." He told me that Tom had more than enough down payment money and met every single requirement necessary to assume the WCDF mortgage. He told me I needed to come down as soon as possible and sign the contract for selling the house.

I left work that day and went straight to the Safeway food store. In a small town like Wheatland a large food store like this has several departments, including the town's floral shop. I purchased a dozen red roses for Vangie. I then drove to Haeberle Realty and signed the sales contract for the house. I knew Vangie also had to sign, and I felt the flowers would help *'lubricate the pen'* when I asked her to sign the contract.

Coming home from the real estate office, I handed Vangie the flower bouquet and kissed her. "What are the flowers for?" she asked with a puzzled look.

"Tom Sawyer is buying our house, and they took the offer we made on the house in Garden City." I paused to view her reaction. It was flat... This could be good or bad. I then continued. "I called Bill Elfman and told him I would take the job."

She did not immediately react to this announcement. Instead, she smelled the flowers and then methodically went to the kitchen, cut the bottom off the stems with a pair of scissors, and put the flowers in a vase. I was dying inside for a reaction of any sort. As she was filling the vase with water she slowly turned and said, "Can we afford to buy the house on Arapaho Street that we liked?"

"We are making $3,500.00 on this house and they are giving us $2,000.00 to move plus paying all moving expenses. We can easily put $5,000.00 down. By using the adjustable-rate mortgage our payment on that house will only be about $30.00 more a month than the payment on this house." I took a breath. "Selling the Saab gets rid of a payment, and we won't have to travel to Cheyenne for everything we need. This will save additional money. We can now easily afford it."

"If you are certain this is what you want to do, I stand by your decision," she replied forthrightly. "By the way, thanks for the flowers, but they weren't necessary." She then gave me a mischievous grin. I immediately melted on the inside. We were very close, but I honestly didn't know what her reaction was going to be in this situation. I was pleased and relieved.

The next few weeks flew by. Tom Sawyer's assumption of the loan on our house in Wheatland went substantially faster than I expected. I had to slow things down a bit to ensure we had a home to move into when we arrived in Kansas. However, the process there went quickly also. We coordinated the house's closing in Wheatland with the moving company so that the day we closed, we could drive straight to Garden City and our household goods would be waiting for us to move into the Arapaho house.

The hardest part of leaving Wheatland was saying goodbye to everyone. We were in Wheatland from January of 1978 to May of 1982. This was the longest time we had stayed anywhere, and it was tough saying goodbye to Nick, Bernadette, Milt, and Marie Marquette. We had also grown close to Pastor Little and his wife. However, we did not drag it out. We simply said our goodbyes and hit the road.

It was the first time we had driven to Garden City. The three-hour trip to Denver always seemed fast. The six-hour trip from Denver to Garden City took several weeks, *or at least felt that way.* Denver to Limon, Colorado was all interstate travel and wasn't too bad. However, the journey from Limon to Hugo, Hugo to Kit Carson, Kit Carson to Eads, and then Eads to Lamar was never-ending and almost painful.

After Lamar you passed through Holly and Granada, Colorado before crossing into Kansas. Once you cross the border on Highway 50 into Kansas, you have another series of one-horse towns not unlike Hugo, Kit Carson, Eads, Lamar, Holly, and Granada. They were Syracuse, Lakin, and Deerfield.

Every one of these small towns seemed to be nothing more than speed traps solely meant to impede arrival at your destination. It didn't matter what your destination, they were impediments to arriving there. It was easy to understand how a hamster feels while running on its wheel. No matter how fast you go the view never seems to change.

Fortunately, Sunflower was paying for up to two weeks of hotel time at the Hilton Inn in Garden City allowing new employees time to get moved into a home. We were only in the Hilton for four days. We closed on the Arapaho house on the third day we were in town with the movers unloading and unpacking on the fourth day. It was a blur, a total, complete blur of activity.

I look back on it, and it still seems like we were *suddenly* no longer in Wheatland. We were now in Garden City, Kansas. This relocation fell into place like a dream in the dark of night where a surreal timeframe passes instantly. We blinked and our lives once again changed forever.

CHAPTER 3
HOLCOMB POWER STATION

Garden City reminded us of Cheyenne, Wyoming. There was a fair amount of shopping and restaurants, and it seemed like it could be a comfortable place to live. Our arrival in May of 1982 was during an extremely active weather season for Finney County and western Kansas.

The tornado sirens in the Indian Hills subdivision blew regularly throughout spring and summer. As soon as the sirens commenced their soulful wail, we quickly herded the kids to the basement and tuned into the local TV channel for instructions.

Initially the kids were terrified at the eerie pitch of the sirens. We spoke calmly while working to engage and entertain them, ensuring everything was fine. It didn't take many trips to the basement before the kids took it all in stride. The thunder, driving rain, and hail that often accompanied the sirens became second nature to them.

Our very first "friend" in Garden City was a meteorologist on the local TV station. He was in his late 50's or early 60's and his name was, believe it or not, *Weatherman Bowman*. I was told by more than one person that he legally changed his first name to Weatherman. Indeed, anytime you saw him on TV his name was displayed as *"Weatherman Bowman."*

We never met him in person, but that spring after moving to Garden City we saw him as much as we saw anyone else. He constantly broke into local programming providing severe thunderstorm and tornado watches and warnings. It seemed like this was daily for weeks after moving there. To this day the magnificent, menacing displays of lightning occurring almost daily in Garden City still stand out as the most incredible we have ever experienced.

The second day we were in town I went to the Garden City office of Sunflower Electric to get my promised $2,000.00 moving bonus check from Gloria Grimes. Gloria was young, attractive, and very petite. She was the human resource girl that we dealt with during the move and, as it turns out, was *very gullible.*

I entered the foyer of the large brick office building and asked the receptionist to see Gloria Grimes. A few minutes later, Gloria walked out and shook my hand. She could not have weighed more than 90 pounds. I had never met her in person before. She seemed like a nice girl.

"Pleased to meet you, Mark." She extended her tiny hand to me. "We at Sunflower are so pleased you decided to come on board after all."

"You say that now…" I smiled coyly as I let my voice intentionally trail off.

"Nonsense, your references were glowing. We checked you out!" She had a twinkle in her eye. "Unfortunately, your bonus check for moving to Garden City has not been cut yet. Could you come back in about an hour to pick it up?"

I grimaced slightly before answering. "I am going to the Holcomb Plant now to check-in. I am excited about starting work there. Can my wife, Vangie, pick it up?"

Gloria looked at me quizzically. "That would be fine…" Her voice then took on an air of concern. "That's a lot of money… How will I know it's her?" Her response surprised me. Had she never heard of, say… A driver's license? *I just couldn't let this pass.*

I kept a straight face and immediately said, "She is easy to spot, she doesn't have any arms." Gloria started laughing. I stared directly at her and never showed an ounce of emotion.

"No, I am serious. It was a birth defect. She doesn't have arms." Gloria stopped laughing and stared at me for a moment. I stared right back at her with a straight face. Her pretty, petite face turned crimson red.

"How does she drive, then?" she asked unbelievingly, still hoping she could laugh this off.

"Our car is equipped with foot controls. She is amazing. She doesn't let anything slow her down. Believe me when I tell you that if someone with arms can do anything, she can do it also. She is an incredible girl." Gloria realized that I was serious and if possible, turned even more crimson. She almost glowed.

She lowered her head slowly, and remorsefully said, "I see. I am sorry I made light of her situation."

"Don't worry about it!" I replied cheerfully. "It is not an issue. Just make sure she gets that check because we are closing on our new house tomorrow morning and we need the money."

I then left for the plant to check-in. *It seems I forgot to mention to Vangie that I may have set her up.* A couple of hours later Vangie arrived at the office and asked to see Gloria Grimes.

"Who shall I say is here to see her?" The receptionist asked appropriately.

"Vangie Gregg. I am here to pick up our moving bonus check."

The receptionist stared at her for a moment and then, barely suppressing her mirth, called Gloria and said, "Gloria, you must come out here. Mrs. Gregg is here to see you."

Gloria walked out, took one look at Vangie and began laughing. Vangie wasn't sure what was happening. She tried to look down and see if she had a wardrobe malfunction. At about that same moment, many of the other girls in the office stepped out and started laughing.

"Please forgive us!" Gloria cupped Vangie's hands as she laughed. "Your husband convinced us you didn't have any arms, and you drove using foot controls in your car."

"He's going to pay for this!" Vangie replied, exasperated, and shaking her head.

"I don't blame you," Gloria replied, still laughing. "He was quite convincing."

Vangie continued. "I try and warn people not to believe anything he says." They all laughed together before Gloria gave her the moving-expense check.

Vangie still brings this up on occasion. Luckily, it is more humorous to her now than it was then.

Check-in at the plant revealed that Curt, Bill, and Brad

hired five experienced Shift Supervisors. I was the third out of

350 MW Holcomb Station

the five. Ultimately, there was Roy Minor, John Russock, Myself, Ray Clyborn, and Dan Coleman.

Roy appeared to have one goal in life... To take over as Operations Manager at Holcomb plant regardless of who he must destroy to get there. I only met his wife once. She was not his original wife and appeared older than him. The only time I met her, she did not seem like a happy woman. No surprise there.

John Russock was a thin, lanky, curly-headed fellow in his late forties or early fifties and one of the easiest-going men

44

I ever worked with. He also came from the south. Unlike Roy, he was blessed with a demeanor and countenance that allowed him to get along with anyone. He didn't portray himself as a smart man, but he wasn't dumb, either. He was the most likable of all the initial hires. He was between wives at this moment in his life... *Nothing unusual for a shift-working power plant operator.*

Ray Clyborn, as near as I could tell was a total buffoon. He claimed to have a huge amount of power plant experience but didn't really seem to know anything of value, or at least that I could discern. Ray regularly stated to the Shift Supervisors his reason for being in Garden City was to hide-out from his latest wife. He claimed he had been married five times and apparently wife number five was not happy with his indiscretions and was looking for him, possibly with a firearm. I have no idea if this was true because I do not believe the man could tell the truth under any circumstance.

Dan Coleman was in his late 30s and a Vietnam veteran. From day − 1, he had all the makings of a misanthrope. Other than his interview, Dan never had a positive thing to say about anything or anyone. His ability to turn a good situation into a bad one was uncanny and continuous.

He began his career in the power industry at a small municipal plant in Nebraska and then worked on the start-up of one of the Craig units in Colorado before coming to Holcomb Station. At this time; none of us had any idea that he still had PTSD issues from Vietnam and went ballistic when under pressure.

PTSD *and* a misanthrope. Plus, he wasn't the quickest thinker. I guess you could say he was the trifecta for the most

45

irritating Shift Supervisor I ever met. Roy Minor was on the list, but Dan topped it.

These men were now my peers. Together we were responsible for commissioning the 350 MW Holcomb Station. The plant was a nice facility but the engineering issues under the nice blue facade were massive. Any engineering problems we experienced at Laramie River Station paled compared to the Holcomb Station's issues.

Besides the engineering issues, the construction management was terrible, with several people losing their lives during the construction phase.

One of the many casualties happened close to me a few weeks after I began employment at the plant. I was chasing piping and looking for potential, future mechanical issues. Wanting to get out of the congested, construction-littered plant and see the sun, I exited one of the west side boiler room doors into the incessant Kansas wind. A few steps from the door I heard a loud clanging and banging sound. It was muffled but got louder and more pronounced. I turned and looked back just in time to see a construction worker fall to the ground no more than 10' from me.

The banging and clanging sounds were from his tool belt and tools slamming into beams as his body fell from the steel girders high above. The siding was incomplete on this side of the plant and a fickle gust of Kansas wind knocked him off balance. He was not tethered as required and fell several floors, straining himself through the beams.

Unlike what you might experience in a movie or TV show, he was still partially conscious when he hit the ground. He was bleeding profusely from his nose and mouth and had at least two compound fractures, one on his arm and one on his leg. He was writhing in pain and screaming incoherently as I ran over to help him.

Several different two-way radio sets were used on the plant site during construction. The Engineering department used one set, different construction firms used another set, operations had another set, and there may have been one or two more sets used by various vendors. The control room personnel monitored the different radios and radio frequencies and, when an emergency was declared, would coordinate the emergency response.

I ran over to him in horror realizing his desperate condition. I immediately followed the protocol for a life-threatening emergency by calling the control room. I announced the emergency slowly and clearly requesting an immediate ambulance. I clearly and carefully elicited our location. The control room acknowledged my call and then followed their protocol to announce the emergency on the different frequencies after calling the EMTs and ambulance.

I was trying to comfort the poor man, but he was in bad shape and incoherent. It seemed like hours, but just a few minutes later I caught a glimpse of the ambulance on the main plant road in front of the plant. It sped by my relative position going east. I immediately called the control room and announced the ambulance had missed us and was going east on the main plant road. The control room acknowledged and quickly went to another frequency to find out what was happening.

A moment later, the radio cracked loudly. "The ambulance is with the accident victim."

"The ambulance is NOT with the accident victim!" I retorted loudly on the radio. "I am with the accident victim and there is no ambulance here!" The radio went silent as the operator switched frequencies to get information.

The radio sprang back to life, "I have verified that the ambulance is with the accident victim!"

It then dawned on all of us at about the same moment. There must have been two accidents that happened at the same time. Sure enough. The continuous and unpredictable Kansas wind knocked two people off the boiler steel simultaneously. The other victim only fell about 4 feet and broke his ankle. My victim was mortally injured.

I stayed with him until the ambulance took him away. It was a difficult day to say the least. Unfortunately, this was not my first brush with death at Holcomb Station. I didn't know it at the time, but there was more carnage ahead.

CHAPTER 4
NEW LIFE, NEW FRIENDS

Not far from the Indian Hills subdivision on Campus Drive was First Assembly of God Church. It was a modern brick facility with a large, detached gymnasium and classrooms. The parking lot was large, and on the back side of the facility were several older, repainted school buses used in their bus ministry. This was our initial attraction to the Church due to our experience with the bus ministry in Wheatland.

Oddly, Vangie and I's first Sunday at First Assembly of God in Garden City was the very first Sunday for the new Pastors of the Church, Gordon and Lois Nelson. Gordon was a small, plucky, intense man who had been a Pastor for many years. He lived in a chiseled, starched suit and was continuously ready to interject exhortations about the Lord. His general intensity was offset by a silly sense of humor.

Lois was the consummate Pastor's wife. She was loving, empathetic, and much like her husband, always dressed to the gills. She wore a fierce, highly sweet perfume. You would smell her coming 30 minutes before you ever saw her. She always wore bright red rouge on her cheeks and absolutely loved to hug people. Everyone who knew her quickly realized she was an *aggressive* hugger. She and her scrappy husband were immensely committed to the Lord and furthering the Gospel. Their 'Churchy' persona was almost cliché, but they were genuine in their zeal and commitment to God and their love of people.

We immediately had a common bond because we started at First Assembly the same Sunday morning that Gordon and

Lois did. Gordon and Lois took an instant liking to Vangie, the kids, and me. The first week we were there they invited us over for dinner. We connected with them on many different levels.

We were excited about the Church because of its dedication to the bus ministry. In those days, an extensive background check of a Church worker was usually no more than dinner with the Pastor. We obviously passed because Gordon and Lois wanted us to get involved with the Youth Group. While we agreed to attend the Youth Group meetings, we also wanted to be involved with the bus ministry.

Garden City was the recipient of a substantial Vietnamese refugee population, many of them working for Iowa Beef Processors (IBP) in the newly built Holcomb facility. The Church capitalized on this by putting together an extensive and effective bus ministry. The buses would travel the town and especially the transient neighborhoods, providing indiscriminate transportation to the Church on Sunday mornings and Wednesday evenings. Sunday was for Church and Sunday School. Wednesday evening was for Royal Rangers and Missionettes. The Youth Group met on Monday evenings. Every age group was covered during the Sunday, Monday, and Wednesday services.

The Vietnamese community in Garden City loved the Church. It got the kids out of the parent's hair for a couple hours on Wednesday and Sunday and provided an added benefit of helping the kids learn English. The kids would in turn, go back home and help their parents with English. The Church was fulfilling the objective of spreading the Gospel. It was a perfect arrangement.

To this point in Vangie and I's spiritual quest we were very naïve and did not realize that one of the biggest problems with Christianity were well-meaning but sorely misdirected Christians. In our wildest imaginations, we could not possibly foresee what we were about to become completely entangled in. However, for now we found what seemed like an idyllic Church home, so much so that I thanked God almost daily for the Church we found.

We were quickly and deeply involved with the bus ministry and the Youth Group. Vangie was driving one of the newer, nicer vans and I was driving an older, larger bus. As with any volunteer endeavor, getting involved revealed gaps and holes that not readily seen at the onset. The four buses and two vans were not being maintained properly. Since I was on day shift for many months at the plant, Vangie and I volunteered to maintain the buses. We didn't do heavy maintenance or oil changes, we just had to keep track of what needed to be done and work out the logistics with the repair shops. We also cleaned and gassed the buses and vans. The weekly cleaning required at least a couple of hours.

We began attending the Youth Group on Monday evenings. Terry and Brenda Elgin were the volunteer Youth Pastors. The Elgins were pillars of the First Assembly in Garden City. The grandma and grandpa, the mom and dad, the brothers, sisters, in-laws, cousins (first, second, and third), and aunts and uncles all seemed to be there. It appeared there were more people related in that Church than were not related.

Terry was an outgoing, red-headed, freckle-faced farmer with a pseudo afro hairdo. Brenda was pretty, reserved, and easy to like. They had kids about the same age as our kids. It seemed the Elgin clan was well-to-do and huge benefactors of the First Assembly of God Church.

Besides being the volunteer Youth Pastor, Terry was also a musician and often led Sunday morning worship. His desire was to distance himself from the youth ministry and concentrate on the worship and music services. His biggest desire in the early days of our friendship was to promote Christian music. Indeed, while we were there, he successfully arranged city-wide concerts with several prominent Christian artists of the day, including Leon Patillo and Farrell and Farrell, both dynamic contemporary Christian artists in the early to mid-1980s.

It was only a few weeks into attending the Monday night youth meetings that Terry and Pastor Nelson turned over the CA's (Christ's Ambassadors) youth group to Vangie and I. Terry and Brenda seemed happy to be free of it. However, Pastor Nelson renamed the CA's "Youth Alive." A simple and due name change, but old traditions apparently die hard. At the time we didn't realize this roiled many people at Church. A name change? Really? Unfortunately, *it only got worse from here.*

I labored all week to build sermons for the Monday night meetings. However, the "Youth Alive" group was not just about preaching. It was about having some fun. Fun for kids from 13 to 18 years old. There were always activities.

Once a month, we would have sectional meetings where all the Assembly of God youth groups in Western Kansas would meet at a different church and have contests and play games. It was always a ton of fun as a couple hundred or more youths would come together for music, games, and preaching.

Some weeks we would go to the roller-skating rink and other weeks in the summer, swimming. We tried to arrange activities that everyone could participate in and enjoy.

I relished giving the sermons. I liked challenging the kids to be more Christ-like. I was not super-knowledgeable of the Bible like I probably should have been, but I knew the core tenets of the Christian Faith and tried to inspire the kids to learn these tenets and make good life decisions. The "Youth Alive" group steadily began growing. When Vangie and I took it over it was about 20 kids. It grew to over 80 kids in the time we were doing the youth ministry before things started going south in the Church.

Vangie opened our home 24/7 to those kids. Every time there was a life-threatening tragedy such as losing a boyfriend or girlfriend, or parents who "just don't understand," or feeling too ugly to go to school, or feeling too dumb to go to school, or even feeling too smart to waste time on school, we were there for them. It was tiresome because we had our own two children but spent as much or more time with these kids as we did with our own.

We also dealt with the more serious issues in their lives such as parental strife in their homes, divorce, depression (theirs and/or their parents), and abuse. The kids knew we were there for them. It was common to receive phone calls or a knock on the door in the middle of the night only to hear about life issues that were insurmountable. In some cases, they were, and it was heartbreaking.

We also had a few youths from a group home for the mentally challenged. Mike Boyer was about eighteen and extremely exuberant. His IQ was quite low, but he was high-functioning and could be hilarious without trying. His favorite expression was, "You kilwing me!" He had a mild speech impediment. If I overwhelmed him in any way and he didn't know how to answer, he would say, "You kilwing me, Mock."

One day we were in the Church van taking kids home after an activity. Out of the clear blue, Mike says, "Mock, I ask God if it okay to dwink beer with mogwut wen we have the sex and he sed to me yes Mike you cun dwink beer with mogwut wen you have the sex." Margaret was his girlfriend in the group home. I had heard from people that this group home was very "open" and this behavior was common. I had others in the van, many of them younger who had heard him say this. I knew I had to respond properly.

"Mike," I said carefully and thoughtfully, "You did the right thing asking God if it was right to drink beer and have sex." I paused to choose just the right words. "However, I don't think God said yes to this because you are not old enough to legally buy beer and you should wait until you and Margaret are married to have sex."

He stared intently at me for several seconds and then blurted out, "You kilwing me, Mock!" He then busted out laughing. I didn't know what to say but I decided this would be something to discuss with him later when none of the other youth group kids were around.

The youth ministry was doing very well, and the bus ministry was doing even better. The buses were packed with kids. We would get them singing contemporary praise songs as we ferried them to and from the church and it was like a choir of angels on the buses. I was so caught up in the bus ministry that I even started knocking on doors recruiting kids for Church. Please understand that this was not my strength, and I certainly did not enjoy it. Door knocking reminded me too much of trying to sell Medicare supplement insurance years earlier. I'm certain I still had PTSD from that experience.

As time passed, we became close friends with Terry and Brenda Elgin, as well as Dwayne and Rene Stiles. We were all about the same age. Dwayne was an extrovert and very witty. Much like Vangie, Rene was comely, classy, and reserved. All of us had kids about the same age.

Terry and Dwayne grew up together and were best friends. For many months late in 1982, all three of our families were extremely close. With this closeness, we began to talk about life, Church, God, and kids to each other.

It wasn't long before Vangie and I began falling prey to their complaints about the things that Pastor and Lois Nelson were doing *'incorrectly.'* Renaming the youth group from CA's to Youth Alive was, in their view, sacrilegious. However, this was just the tip of the iceberg. They were quite critical of how he managed the Church finances. They felt he was dumping too much money into the bus ministry that was "only for the Vietnamese kids." They even complained he opened the Sunday morning Church services incorrectly... *Really, what is wrong with the way he opens the services???* This began to transition into things like, "his sermons are just boring and hard to follow."

The problem was, as we drew nearer to the Elgins and Stiles, we were slowly starting to fall into this thinking with them. After all, Terry, Brenda, Dwayne, and Rene were our friends, and we respected them. In fact, we all traveled to Wichita a couple of times to see Christian concerts and visit the big shopping mall. We would spend the night at the Holiday Inn so the kids could play in the pool by our rooms. Looking back, these were very enjoyable times for us. We thoroughly relished being with the Elgins and Stiles.

Pastor Gordon and Lois Nelson continuously warned us about a potential insurrection in the Church. On more than one occasion they discussed how the two previous Pastors at First Assembly were mistreated and "run out of the Church." They were hoping they could "reign in this spirit of rebellion" and get this Church back to where it should be.

The most recent former Pastor, Leland Dillon, started another Church about three miles up Campus Drive from First Assembly. Many of the former members of the First Assembly migrated to his Church. Yet, even knowing there was a history of problems of this sort, we were taken in by the negative views of the Elgins and Stiles. Terry was a compelling speaker and an excellent candidate for a professional debate team or a political career. However, this does not excuse the fact that we were allowing this negativity to slowly poison us.

Their issues with Gordon and Lois Nelson began to conflict with Vangie and me because we both thought highly of them. We generally felt they were doing a great job at Church. However, the constant negativity of the Stiles and Elgins slowly took its toll.

The Bible speaks of "a little yeast leavening the entire loaf." At the time we couldn't see this 'yeast' was permeating our relationship with the Elgins. Furthermore, we didn't realize it was leavening the entire loaf… _Including us_.

Things were about to change on many fronts. The plant put us on shift work. This meant I was tired and grumpy much of the time and had to do the youth group and bus ministry as my schedule permitted... And I was usually exhausted. It also began to limit our time with the Stiles and Elgins. While this was a blessing in disguise, much damage was already done.

CHAPTER 5
POWER PLANT OR TRAIN WRECK?

My life away from the Holcomb Plant was extremely busy and fulfilling. My life at the plant was a different story. Only a week or so after I started, the new Control Room Operators were coming on board. They were an eclectic and rag-tag bunch, not unlike the shift supervisors.

To me, there was only one of them worth hiring, and his name was Don Unger. He and his wife Denise and their two children, Nathan and Noelle, came from Pennsylvania Electric Company. They purchased a nice, higher-end home a mile away from Indian Hills.

Don worked at Keystone Station prior to coming to Holcomb. It was a massive, two-unit, 1600 MW plant that used CE super-critical boilers and Westinghouse turbines and generators. Holcomb was a B&W sub-critical boiler with a G.E. turbine and generator. Though he was very smart, Don came on board with much to learn due to the differences in the plants.

Don and I hit it off right away. He was a few years older than me and sported an odd Dutch-boy haircut. Don was an introvert and could be very prickly when he interacted with people. He had an arrogance about him that was an immediate turn-off. Denise was a pretty, dark-haired girl and she and Don seemed like a nice couple. Don was emphatically not a Christian. He was raised Catholic but at some point in his life he rebelled and decided it was all "hogwash."

After the final Control Room Operator started work at the Holcomb Station, the Shift Supervisors spent an afternoon haggling over which control room operator each of us would take on their shift. One of the five new control room operators was a very tall, freckle-faced man named Joe Gomez. He was a hulking guy and had the largest ears I have ever seen on any human being. The moment you met him you could hardly help but to stare. His freckles were red and oddly uniform in placement and size. They worked together with the strong tint of red in his hair to complement his extremely extroverted personality. However, those massive ears were truly something to behold.

Joe seemed to know very little about power plants. He had been a contract operator doing system alignments at a nuclear plant start-up. He didn't operate anything on the nuclear side. He just performed auxiliary operator work. As near as I could tell by talking to him, someone would simply tell him exactly which valve to open or close and he would manhandle it. No thinking involved, just muscle and sweat. This was certainly a job he seemed well suited for. However, moving beyond this to being a control room operator? No way. Absolutely no way.

During this decision-making meeting of the shift supervisors and control room operators, petite little Gloria Grimes knocked quietly on the conference room door and then came in saying, "I have everyone's paycheck!"

Before anyone could respond, Joe Gomez leaped up and loudly exclaimed, "Hot-dog! The eagle has shit!" Most of us were shocked by his outburst. He impulsively marched over to Gloria and said, "lay it on me, little mama!" Gloria looked frightened as she hastily sorted through the envelopes to find his check. Joe seemed oblivious to the fact that this was offensive to Gloria and others in the room.

Just like choosing who would be on your ball team as a child, someone had to be picked last. Joe was the last picked because no Shift Supervisor wanted Joe as their Control Operator. We could not figure out why Curt, Bill, and Brad even hired him. Fortunately, Roy Minor decided this would be an excellent moment to showcase his obviously superior skills. He chose Joe with open arms as if he were his long-lost brother or son. Later Roy elicited to all of us that he "would be the man to make a *real* operator out of Joe."

Roy's choice of Joe Gomez put even more focus on moving into Brad's job, and he proved he would stop at nothing to get it. Roy took open shots at Brad at every turn. It did not matter what Brad did or said, Roy would find fault in it and advertise openly that Brad was a know-nothing, inexperienced idiot who was only holding his position because of his ties with the equally worthless Curt.

During the crazy bargaining session to choose Control Room Operators, I argued hard for Don Unger and got him. I think everyone recognized Don as the sharpest of the Control Room Operators, but he wasn't well-liked because of his bristly demeanor. His personality didn't bother me because we seemed to get along well. I was determined to fix his negative life attitude. There was something missing in him, and I wanted him to figure out there was an absence of Christ in his life.

Don and I immediately began carpooling together. The drive from the east side of Garden City to the plant was about 30 minutes. We would talk the entire round trip each day. I would engage him about his faith, or lack thereof. We fully discussed that the real meaning of Christianity was forgiveness from Christ's ultimate sacrifice. A man without sin who willingly gave Himself for the forgiveness of all. It is a simple but complex subject that a person either understands or rejects.

I wore him down. He, Denise, and the kids agreed to attend Church with us. They were touched. He began to understand and feel there was something to what I was saying. We became close friends. Vangie and Denise were also getting along well.

Besides discussing Christ, we continuously hashed out the daily problems at the plant. We both fully agreed the plant was a total mess, the plant construction management was terrible, the design issues were virtually insurmountable, and the Holcomb Management team was going helter-skelter without discernible direction. Also, neither one of us could stand Dan Coleman. We had to follow his shift and deal with the crap he would put forth daily. I had multiple meltdowns about Dan Coleman's actions on the trip back to Garden City with Don being a captive audience.

Curt finally found and hired the new Holcomb Maintenance Manager. His name was Dale Warnky, and he was from the J.M. Stuart Station which was owned by Dayton Power and Light. It was a huge, multi-unit, 2300 MW plant with super-critical boilers and a massive batch of operational problems. It was considered a "maintenance run plant." This is what we called plants when the operation's department was subservient to the maintenance department. To me, this was the tail wagging the dog. It made no sense for operations to be subservient to maintenance. It should be the other way around or at least a team effort.

Dale openly and verbally *HATED* operators. He acted like he was joking when he said things such as, "Operators are the root of all evil." However, he would say it with venom, and it was easy to see through his facade. There was absolutely no doubt that he truly loathed operators and the entire operations department from the very first moment he came on-site. It didn't matter what happened in the plant. It was always the operator's fault in his eyes.

Curt would constantly laugh off our complaints about Dale like they were nothing. Even Dale's operational counterpart, Bill Elfman, could not stand working with him and seethed at the mention of his name. Of course, Brad sided with Curt on every issue, so Dale was not considered obnoxious or counter-productive to Brad simply because Curt liked him.

Dale was a very heavy, large-framed guy with a perfectly round face and a bone structure resembling a cartoon pig. It only took us a short time to openly nickname him Porky Pig. Every passing day we discussed the latest antics of Porky Pig. We were certain he heard us referring to him as Porky because he became more belligerent by the day and aggressively tried to make the Shift Supervisor's job as difficult and frustrating as possible.

Porky was responsible for hiring the plant maintenance personnel. He went out of his way to find people molded in his own image. We joked about the test for employment in the Holcomb maintenance department having only one question... "Do you hate operators with all of your heart, soul, and mind?" If the answer was "Yes!" You were immediately hired. It made no difference if you knew anything about maintenance or power plants. In fact, the original maintenance force at Holcomb had little or no power plant experience.

Curt Burn's boss was a man named Raymond Hemmings. He worked for years at the small gas-fired power plant in Garden City but was anointed as the Generation Manager for Sunflower when they started construction on the Holcomb Plant. He was comically the wrong man for any position of authority.

To me, his personal attributes for this lofty position included a minimal IQ, no power plant understanding, no leadership abilities, and no public (or individual) speaking abilities. I realize now that my views were mean, obnoxious, and seasoned from minimal maturity on my part. However, it doesn't mean they were necessarily wrong.

During the days before we started shift work at the plant, we quickly figured out who to trust and who to avoid. It became painfully obvious that Roy Minor was trouble. His crew members were intensely loyal to him because they were young and inexperienced, and he convinced them he was God's gift to power plants. His intense hatred for Brad and Curt and his burning aspiration to wrest either of their jobs reached a crescendo early in the start-up. He was openly challenging their authority, their decisions, and their leadership.

Brad and Curt reached the point in their relationship with Roy Minor where they invited him to shape up *or resign*. He finally saw the handwriting on the wall and began sending resumes' in every direction. He also gave up on making Joe

Gomez a knowledgeable operator and put enough pressure on him that he quit. This was probably Roy's single best (and only) contribution to the plant. Joe wasn't a bad guy; he just should not have been hired as a Control Room Operator.

You could depend on Dan Coleman to always view anything negatively. Someone could tell him he won the lottery and hand him $1,000,000.00 dollars cash and he would immediately start cursing the government because of the chunk they were taking, and he would assure you that someone would undoubtably rob him before the day's end. He could not see anything positive if his life depended on it. He was a true, textbook *misanthrope*.

Dan Coleman's PTSD issues became obvious when any pressure was on him. He would flip out. It was more than just a temperament issue; he would instantly transition from dead-calm to ballistic. I don't know how it was possible, but I began to like him less and less as time passed. He had absolutely no respect for me, mostly due to my age and the fact that when he opened his mouth and said something stupid, I would openly check him on it. I may have been extremely immature and obnoxious, but I also knew a fair amount about the plant that he didn't know.

The control room operators had minimal experience, and the remaining auxiliary operators were hired off the street with no experience whatsoever. Part of getting the governmental buy-in to build the plant was a promise that most of the workers would be hired directly off the streets of western Kansas. The Shift Supervisors were then responsible for all training and preparation of their crew members to operate the plant. I loved this. I enjoyed training my people.

Once we started to shift work, but before the plant was in service, I would do things like kill all the incoming power from the switchyard and then make my operators recover from this 'black plant' situation. I would assure them it was far more thrilling and even terrifying when this kind of thing happened with the plant operating.

Dan Coleman would play a game with his crew that he named, "Stump the Dummy." They would walk around the plant with Dan pointing at something, asking one of his crew members what it was, and how it worked. If they didn't answer to his liking, he would scathingly belittle them in front of their peers. He felt peer embarrassment would compel them to learn their jobs. I'm not sure it fomented their desire to learn as much as it did their intense urge to kill him and then tell God he died.

As near as we could tell, Roy Minor trained his people by telling them stories about how amazing he was at Spurlock, his previous plant. He had the foresight to make them read the vendor's manuals, but I am not sure this had any training value. The vendor's equipment manuals are not intended to be training manuals, just technical references. You could glean information from them if you had a previous understanding of the equipment. However, these were new and completely inexperienced people. They needed more than a reference manual.

During all these personnel issues we attempted start-up activities with the contract start-up group from United Engineers and Constructors (UE&C). One of their lead start-up engineers was Hugh Mayer. Hugh was a flaming alcoholic and wholly incompetent in his role as a start-up engineer. However, we had to push forward with start-up activities regardless of personnel issues, whether on their part or our part.

During a dayshift in the early part of the plant commissioning process, we were supposed to "bump" the pulverizer motors to ensure they were wired properly and spinning the proper direction. The motors were not yet coupled to the pulverizers, allowing us to do this safely. Working with Hugh, I went to the 4160 Volt circuit breaker room with a couple of my operators. I was on the radio with two different people. The first was Don Unger, my control room operator, and the other was a UE&C start-up engineer in the burner management room. He was instructing a plant instrument tech on how to properly use logic bypasses (wire jumpers) to allow a pulverizer motor to start.

The procedure was improperly planned, and poorly executed by the UE&C start-up personnel. The result was an explosion and the total devastation of one of our high voltage, main electrical busses.

Luckily, we were far enough away from the circuit breakers that we were not injured or burned. It was quite a conflagration that should never have happened. We were lucky no one was killed and/or severely burned. Several hundred thousand dollars of damage was incurred in just a few seconds of time in this incident.

Several days after recovering from the destruction of our 4160 V bus, we began the arduous task of flushing all the major systems to clean the piping and vessels. The first major system flushed was the hotwell and condensate system.

At Hugh's direction, we filled the hotwell and started the first hotwell pump. We had water recirculating back to the condenser (as it should) while Hugh was checking the vibration levels and motor amps on the hotwell pump. For some reason, he decided the packing needed to be "burned-in."

He tightened the pump's stuffing box so tight that it filled the plant with smoke and destroyed the shaft on the pump. I smelled the pungent smoke up by the control room and ran downstairs to the hotwell pump, only to see the thick, acrid, smoke rolling out of the pump shaft. I screamed at Hugh several times to trip the pump. Unfortunately, he was drunk and wouldn't change course. I had to go around Hugh and order the control room to trip the motor on the hotwell pump. His actions ruined the shaft and the pump. This was a measly $50,000.00 to $75,000.00 dollar mistake. Nothing major.

In another colossal failure just a week or so later, he instructed the control room operator on another shift to start one of the enormous circulating water pumps at the cooling tower. The circulating water pumps supply all the cooling water to the main plant condenser. They move hundreds of thousands of gallons of water per minute from the cooling tower through the 78-inch diameter supply lines to the condenser. From the condenser tubes, the flow is back through the 78-inch diameter return lines to the top of the cooling tower where the heated water drops through the "fill" or packing in the tower, causing evaporation and cooling. This cooling flow is non-ending when the plant is running.

Hugh instructed the Control Room Operator to start one of the huge circulating water pumps WITHOUT FILLING THE SUPPLY OR RETURN LINES. These pipes are over 6' in diameter and more than a quarter of a mile long as they connect the remote cooling tower to the condenser in the plant. A person can walk, unencumbered, through this 6' diameter piping due to its enormity. When the circulating water pump started, it created a massive, killer wave inside the piping that we call "water hammer."

This enormous water hammer slammed into one of the elbows in the underground line and blew it apart, immediately forming a 25' deep and 75' wide sinkhole that would swallow a large semi-truck and trailer. This was Hugh's last screw-up. He was fired by UE&C management. Unfortunately, his replacement wasn't much better. The plant start-up was behind schedule and over budget, and things were deteriorating daily... *Especially on the personnel side of the plant.*

Not long after he was hired, Dale Warnky convinced Curt that the Shift Supervisors should no longer have access to the administration building on back shifts and weekends. We were stripped of our key to the admin building. This was a personal affront to every Shift Supervisor. We could no longer get to the shop tools. We could no longer get to the food and soda vending machines. We could no longer get to the shower rooms. Dale Warnky, in effect, looked at the Shift Supervisors and said *gotcha*!

We complained bitterly to Bill Elfman and Brad Schultz to no avail. We even cited that it was a fire and safety concern because if the fire sprinkler system tripped for any reason, the admin building would flood without us being able to stop it. The fire system block valves for the admin building were in the breezeway and could no longer be accessed at night and on weekends.

Bill Elfman did not agree with taking the keys away from us. However, his hands were tied. Curt, Brad, and Dale felt we didn't need to have the keys. *The entirely irritating part of this was nothing happened that would have prompted this action.* Maybe if someone had violated the sanctity of the admin building or abused the privilege of having access, it would have made more sense. No, it was nothing like this. Dale just wanted to stick it to the operations department.

On my next graveyard shift, I reverted to the grossly immature and vindictive child who almost got fired at LRS. The plant, of course, was not running yet, so we had tons of time on our hands. Essentially, we were just training ourselves on the backshift while doing actual start-up activities on the day and afternoon shifts. Graveyards were boring and difficult to stay awake. Therefore, I decided that it was time to return the favor to Porky for all he was doing for us.

I grabbed Don Unger and a couple of the heftier auxiliary operators and we removed the door from the breezeway. We also removed the door from Dale's office. We carefully turned his desk on its side, his bookcases on their side, and everything else in his office sideways. We weren't done yet. We also filled every square inch of his office with the vending machines that we could no longer access in the admin building.

With incredible difficulty, we carefully reinstalled his door and the breezeway door. The locks, of course, were seriously damaged because you can't remove a door without being inside. We couldn't get inside (properly) because we didn't have keys.

The shift change was at 0700 every morning, but we always relieved 15 to 20 minutes early. Luckily, I cleared the front gate before Curt, Brad, and Porky arrived. It is my understanding that Porky went fully unhinged. So much so that he wanted to call the Holcomb police department and file a police report. Curt, thankfully, talked him out of this. Me, Don, and the auxiliary operators took a vow of silence and pleaded absolute ignorance. This issue caused a rift in the front office so extreme that none other than Raymond Hemmings, Curt's boss, got involved.

That next evening after I arrived for work an older blue Ford sedan pulled into the admin building. It was Raymond. He told the guard at the front gate to call and ask me to come to his car. After making my way down from the control room, I stood by his driver's window as he asked me, "What do you think the problem is at this plant?" I was stunned. I had never seen him at the plant before, and now he shows up at night to ask me a question through his car window. Really? He was just an odd duck. I was frustrated enough with the entire situation that I decided to tell him how I really felt.

"Dale Warnky, the Maintenance Manager, hates the operations department and goes out of his way to cause us problems." I was trying to keep my emotions to a minimum and just give him facts. This was difficult because I was angry. I continued. "For no reason that I know of, he convinced Curt to take away our keys to the admin building. This is not a good thing because we cannot even get to the fire system block valves."

He just stared at me with a blank, dull stare before saying, "I will see what I can do. I must go now." He then rolled up his car window, backed out of the parking spot and drove away. That was it. There was no further investigation into the "break-in" in Porky's office.

The next evening, when I arrived for shift change, Dan Coleman gave me a key to the Admin Building. All five Shift Supervisors got their keys back. There was never any further discussion about Porky's office whatsoever. This is a good thing. Had they investigated it hard enough, it would have cost me my job. While I didn't specifically read it in the personnel guide, I am certain breaking and entering is considered an egregious breach of work rules... *Even if you worked there.*

The strain in the working relationship between Dan Coleman and I reached the inevitable conclusion. Dan hated the Holcomb Plant, Brad, Curt, me, and everyone. His crew hated him. I followed his shift on most days and had to listen to his constant and continuous complaining about everything. I was sick of it.

One afternoon, when I came in to relieve him, he had painfully spent the day dealing with the pressure of the start-up and the incompetence of the UE&C Start-up Engineers. He was in fine form and started railing on everything and everybody. I finally heard enough and reached my limit of tolerance.

I rudely interrupted his tirade. "Dan, if this place is so bad, why don't you leave and go to another plant?"

He looked at me angrily. "I would leave this @%$!!# place in a heartbeat if I had someplace to go!"

I immediately removed my wallet and took out a phone number for the Bonanza Plant in Vernal, Utah. I always kept up with who was building new plants in the hiring phase. I dialed the number for Deseret G&T, the company building the plant. It rang a few times, and a man with a very professional voice answered.

"Bonanza Plant operations, this is Stan."

"Stan, my name is Dan Coleman. I am a Shift Supervisor here at the Holcomb Station in western Kansas. I heard you might be hiring Shift Supervisors. Is this the case?"

"As a matter of fact, we are. I am the Operations Superintendent, and we are currently interviewing for shift supervisors and assistant shift supervisor positions. Are you interested?"

Dan went wide-eyed as I continued the conversation, pretending to be him. "Yes, yes, I am. I started at a municipal plant in Nebraska and then worked on the start-up of the Craig Plant and I am now here starting the 350 MW Holcomb Station. Can you tell me something about the Bonanza Plant?"

"We are a 450 MW unit with a Foster Wheeler Boiler and a Westinghouse Turbine. We will use a baghouse and a state-of-the-art wet scrubber. Are you still interested?" Stan seemed like a pleasant, knowledgeable guy.

"Absolutely. Could I get your address? I will send my resume'."

"Certainly, I am very interested in seeing it and talking to you in the future, Dan."

We exchanged information, and I hung up the phone. Dan was still wide-eyed and shaking his head in disbelief. "Dan," I said authoritatively, "Bonanza Plant is a 450 MW unit, and they are interviewing for Shift Supervisors. You should send him your resume as soon as possible."

"I can't believe you just did that!" Dan exclaimed, half in anger and half in disbelief.

"Hey, they are hiring! What have you got to lose? Send them a damn resume."

We finished shift turnover. Dan went dark on me, saying little else before leaving for home. I went to the control room and told Don and my operators, word for word, what happened. They roared in laughter and cheered like I was a rock star. At that time I could not possibly perceive the ramifications of what I just did with Dan. It was beyond imagination. *My days of dealing with Dan were far, far from over.*

As the days passed, the personnel issues kept deteriorating within the operations and maintenance departments at the Holcomb Plant. Infighting and a lack of cooperation were the rule and not the exception throughout the plant. The maintenance personnel hated the operations personnel and vice versa. Dan Coleman hated everything and everybody, and Roy Minor back-stabbed Brad, Curt, Bill, Dale, and all the Shift Supervisors. The Control Room Operators could not get along amongst themselves and the UE&C start-up personnel were proving their incompetence daily while Holcomb Station fell further behind schedule.

Unfortunately, things were also deteriorating rapidly in Garden City with Church issues. Both situations were on a parallel trajectory. It was disheartening and distressful.

One morning, after a depressing graveyard shift, I was completely exhausted. I begrudgingly called the Intermountain Power Plant being built in Delta, Utah. I had called them many months earlier before finding out that Holcomb was hiring. It turns out they were now interviewing for shift supervisors. *I sent them my resume that morning before going to bed.*

CHAPTER 6
INTERMOUNTAIN POWER PROJECT

As difficult as it was with shift work, Vangie and I were still able to maintain our leadership role in the youth group while continuing to work at the plant and support the bus ministry. However, the Church was changing. The quiet murmuring against Pastor's Gordon and Lois Nelson behind closed doors began to transition to open accusations. We didn't realize it then, but we were experiencing the beginning of a Church insurrection.

Gordon and Lois were openly confronted by the Church Board and indicted for poor leadership, substandard preaching, an inability to grow the Church, favoritism, and poor use of Church resources. The weekly collection was down, way down, and they were being accused of an inability to draw people to the Church who had the ability to support it financially. These were code words for the Vietnamese and Mexican children in the bus ministry who weren't bringing in parents with deep pockets.

Much to my embarrassment, I listened to Terry and Dwayne long enough that I was sucked into this heresy. I do not and will not blame Terry and Dwayne for my failure because all I had to do was step back and look openly at the situation and I would have known what was happening. The Church collections were down because the Elgin clan and Stiles clan bonded together and quit giving. This is sometimes referred to as voting with your checkbook in a Church. The favoritism that Gordon and Lois were being accused, was not favoritism at all. It was Gordon's refusal to treat the Elgin clan like royalty. It was his refusal to *NOT* practice favoritism that was causing the real problem.

The poor spending habits he was accused of were simply the continuation of the bus ministry when the giving was down. The bus ministry was an expensive endeavor, and the Elgin/Stiles "faction" in the Church wanted the money turned inward instead of outward.

It is critically important to understand this bus ministry outreach was one of the most powerful Christian ministries in Western Kansas during the early 1980's. The number of souls reached for Christ because of the bus program in the Vietnamese and Hispanic communities was staggering. The First Assembly of God Church was fulfilling the Great Commission that Christ himself tasked the Church to strive for.

Unfortunately, with this success came opposition. Opposition straight from the pits of hell. Stop reading now if it bothers you that I would say this. I now know that it was not a coincidence that we started Church at First Assembly on the same day as Gordon and Lois's first day. I did not know it then, but we had a pivotal but unsuccessful role in what took place over the next several months. My failure to stand up for Gordon and Lois was very costly to them, Vangie and me, and many others.

Rather than take a stand with Gordon and Lois Nelson, I called Intermountain Power Project and ran from my duties at the Holcomb Plant and the Church. At the time, I was convinced that God called Vangie and I to be missionaries to the Mormons in Utah. Now, let us look at this for a moment.

The move to Garden City was inspired by a dream that was both 100% accurate and revealed things to me that I could not have possibly known. I saw the plant and its unique systems before ever seeing them. The immediate sale of the Saab, the house, and everything coming together to get us to Garden City was compelling. What about the voice on Mary Street; *"It cannot be stopped now."*

Now, suddenly, I decided that God called us as missionaries to the Mormons. Did I have any dreams to confirm this? *No.* Was there anything that would indicate God was calling us to Utah, other than Intermountain Power Project was hiring Shift Supervisors? *No.* Did I hear a voice? *No.* Did Gordon and Lois Nelson think this was the right thing to do? I don't know. We had wrongfully distanced ourselves from them due to our friendship with the Elgins and Stiles.

The size increase of the youth group from 20 to over 80, and many of the youth telling me how much they enjoyed my sermons apparently swelled my already fat head to about four times its normal size. I was obviously a spiritual giant destined to do big things, right? Why not take on the entire Mormon Church and show them true Christianity? Obviously, God called us to Utah. *Why else would they be hiring Shift Supervisors there now?*

I look back with total shame and embarrassment, finding it hard to believe I could have been so far off-base. I was led away by my own desires and ambitions that made no sense whatsoever. We were needed at the Church in Garden City and I arbitrarily decided to be a missionary to the Mormons… *Stupid people do stupid things.*

Even though I only had five years of power plant experience, my resume' was good. I commissioned all three units at LRS and had the Four Corners and Bridger experience. While I was obviously a job hopper, my experience in start-ups was excellent. Getting an invitation for an interview was easy.

I decided to take some time off on a graveyard shift and use my long-change to drive to Montrose, leave the kids, and then drive to Delta, Utah for the interview. They were paying all travel expenses for the interview, and missing graveyard shifts was always my preference, so it worked well for us. It was about an 8-hour drive from Garden City to Montrose and another 6-hour drive to Delta.

Delta, Utah was a hole. Its only claim to fame is the former Japanese internment camp located about ten miles west of Delta in a township named Topaz. After the Japanese bombed Pearl Harbor in World War II, the United States rounded-up and imprisoned the Japanese at several internment camps throughout America because they thought they were threats to the country. The internment camp in Topaz was open for three years during WW II and peaked at over 8,000 prisoners.

Delta is in the middle of the desert. And only had about 2000 people prior to the plant construction. There were two restaurants in town; the only churches were Mormon Churches. The plant was about 30 minutes away. However, it was a big, beautiful powerhouse. There was no expense spared at this plant. If you could call a plant a Cadillac, this was it. It was going to be one of the nicest, if not the nicest coal-fired plant in the United States.

Delta did not have any available housing without purchasing property and building a house. There was plenty of this happening by people staffing the plant. Because housing was not readily available to purchase, the Intermountain Power Project built a substantial number of tenement-style apartment buildings to house workers until they could find something more suitable. The apartments were small, high-density, and prefabricated.... *Quite cheaply*. There was no problem renting living space in these massive brown tenements. Rent was minimal for plant personnel, and people were moving through them at a stunning pace.

I interviewed with Gale Chappell, the President of Intermountain Power Service Corporation (IPSC), Bob Daniels, the Operations Manager, and Juan Archuleta, the Training Manager. IPSC was the operating company the Los Angeles Department of Water and Power put in place to operate and maintain the plant.

Gale Chappell was a high-profile plant manager at Utah Power and Light System. Gale was a true powerhouse guy. He worked his way up from janitor to become the Plant Manager of the two largest Utah Power and Light coal-fired plants and then became the President of the newly formed IPSC. He was professional, authoritarian, direct, smart, and probably the perfect pick for his position.

Bob Daniels came from Nevada Power. He had a goofy handlebar mustache that he slathered-on tons of wax to maintain the tightly curled tips. It appeared that he used the same mustache wax on his thinning hair, combing it straight back and greasing it so tightly to his scalp that it looked painted-on. The mustache and hair were combined with wire-rim glasses and a cowboy hat that made him look like a throwback from a collodion wet plate photograph of a cowpoke from the 1880s. He was the Operations Manager at the Reid Gardner Station before coming to IPSC.

Juan Archuleta was a diminutive man who dressed like an ambassador or a member of the royal family. His Spanish accent was so strong, I could barely understand him. He didn't fit the setting. His only qualifications for the training department appeared to be his former experience as a Mormon missionary.

The interview took about one and a half hours. They asked several heavy-duty, technical questions. Gale Chappell was intimidating. He truly understood power plants. There was no mistaking this. His questions were hard, and he knew how to dig for answers to ensure you weren't trying to fake your way through the interview. I wasn't sure how well I did because Gale kept coming back at me in the interview process. I later found out this was his style. He wanted to ensure you were not shallow in your plant understanding. *Apparently, I fooled them anyway.*

Intermountain Power Plant

They told me they planned to hire the original Shift Supervisors and then immediately hire and build their crews entirely with inexperienced local people. The Shift Supervisors would then spend several weeks at the Craig Plant in Craig, Colorado on shift with their new crews training them to properly operate a power plant. They already had all the permissions they needed with Colorado Ute Electric Association, the company that was running the Craig Plant.

When the interview finished, they excused me from the room for an "internal discussion." I was nervous and fidgety because this was an intense experience. Ten minutes later they emerged from their isolation and offered me the Shift Supervisor's job. They wanted an answer as soon as possible. My salary offer was slightly higher than what I was making at Sunflower Electric, and their benefits were better. They paid all moving expenses, including purchasing our house in Garden City if necessary.

With little consideration, I told them yes right there on the spot. I didn't even ask Vangie her opinion. It was probably a good thing. She was entirely underwhelmed with Delta and the area in general. Deep down, she knew that God was not calling us there. However, I was on a roll. She found it difficult to stop me when I fell into this mode.

I was blown away by their proclamation that they would buy our house if it wouldn't sell. They told me there were several conditions associated with the house buyout program. However, just hearing that our house would not be an obstacle was a compelling reason to accept the position.

Once again, at the time I felt this must be God wanting us to be missionaries *because it went so well.* I never considered that it had far more to do with the fact that Delta was a tiny town in the middle of the desert with nothing close to it except the powerplant and the remains of a WWII internment camp. The nearest town of any size was Provo, Utah which was 90 miles northeast. Therefore, finding semi-qualified people to work at this plant was probably challenging.

The trip back to Montrose was a cold one. It was colder inside the car than outside. Vangie was in silent mode. The silence wasn't the bad part; it was 'that' look on her face. The kids later referred to it as "the evil eye." I had already told her about the interview and the training of the operators in Craig and that *I accepted the job.*

After an hour or so of silence, she finally decided to talk to me. "Why would you accept the job without discussing it with me first?" I could tell she was seething.

"I can always change my mind. I just wanted to be decisive. Besides, I think the Lord wants us there." This brought another round of silence for several more miles.

I decided to push the issue and get it over with. "Do you not want to move there?" She just looked at me incredulously.

"The question is, why would YOU want to move there?" Her anger was coming to the surface.

"I think we are supposed to be there." I was firmly maintaining my rhetoric.

"There isn't even a Christian Church in that town. Do you even know where the nearest Church is?"

"Maybe we are supposed to start one?" I kept my eyes on the road. I didn't want to see her face. It didn't matter. I could feel her burning glare. I'm certain it was damaging my skin to the point of causing skin cancer.

"Whatever. You are going to do whatever you want. There is no use me arguing with you about it." It was clear. She was definitely pissed.

"Will you move there with me?" I asked slowly and carefully.

She just looked at me until I acknowledged her glare. "Like I have a choice?" She had resignation in her voice.

"Of course, you have a choice. If you won't move there, we won't move. Period!" I was getting angry now. I was tired of the game.

"Right!" She fired back. "And you will hold this over me for the rest of my life. Let's just move and get it over with. I will make it work." I decided to let things ride. Any further pushing was going to end in a serious fight.

We stayed the night in Montrose and visited our folks. The next morning, we departed for Garden City avoiding any discussion of moving. It wasn't until we arrived home and put the kids to bed that she brought the subject back up.

"Are you putting the house on the market?" I was shocked she even brought it up. She then continued, "if we are moving, we will obviously have to sell it."

"You haven't told me you wanted to move. Why would I consider putting the house on the market?" I was trying not to be argumentative but could not keep the sarcasm from slipping in.

"Look, let's get something straight, *buster*. You already made-up your mind. We both know this. You need to make a plan and stick with it because I need to know what to do." She seemed resolute. After nine years of marriage, I knew where things stood.

"My plan is to have the house on the market while I am at the Craig Plant. This way you are not in Delta alone while I am away in Colorado."

"What if the house sells? What will I do then?" She had a valid point.

"It probably won't sell quickly. We may have to use their home purchase program. If it did sell fast, we would have to adjust the closing until I am back from the Craig Plant and in Delta." She accepted this with resignation, *but at least she accepted it.*

After the interview and their job offer, I became oblivious to work and Church problems. I mentally checked-out of the Holcomb Plant after the interview. Vangie and I called Pastor Nelson and asked to speak to him and Lois together at their house. I never thought this would be as difficult as it was. After arriving and telling them our plans, they were genuinely devastated.

Lois cried deep from her heart as she hugged Vangie tight. I told them we were supposed to be Missionaries in that area. Pastor, in his own direct manner, very bluntly stated, "I certainly hope you both prayed your guts out on this and that you got it right." Even then I knew he didn't believe we were "called" to Delta.

I didn't expect their extreme reaction. We never dreamed we were this important to them. They were genuinely crushed. Looking back, I was so caught-up in my own selfish plans that I couldn't see just how much pressure the Church was putting on them. I could have done so many things better and differently. There are no other words for this other than; *I plain and simple… screwed-up.*

As soon as our house was listed for sale with Neil Mecklenburg, I gave my two weeks' notice at the plant. They were noticeably miffed that I was leaving after less than a year with the largest and most important part of the plant start-up still ahead. I kept my departure as positive as I could, saying it was due to "an amazing offer from an incredible plant that I just can't walk away from…"

Since I was one of the final shift supervisors hired at the Intermountain Plant, they had already hired the non-experienced personnel who were going to the Craig Plant. I was too late to help vet my crew members. However, they did a decent job. I was not displeased with the crew they picked for me.

I drove to Delta and moved into a bottom-floor apartment in the massive brown tenement structure. It was housing many of the newer plant employees that came to Delta from outside the area. The apartment was essentially empty. I was sleeping on the floor in a sleeping bag. There was a refrigerator, so I bought some plastic dinnerware and made the apartment my temporary home prior to traveling to Craig to school the operators in an operating plant environment.

I didn't anticipate how homesick I would become. I had never been away from Vangie and the kids for any length of time before. By the end of the first week, I was missing them so badly that I ached. By the end of the second week, I was second-guessing my decision to come to Delta. I am certain I would have caved and gone home except for the start of my third week, which had us all traveling to Craig, Colorado to start the training of our crews at the Craig Plant.

I left my car in Delta and rode to Craig with another Shift Supervisor, named Steve Johnson. He and I got along well, and the plan was for him to drive on the first shift go-around, and then I would drive the next time. It was a money-saving endeavor, and he was my first attempt at converting someone from Mormonism to Christianity.

Steve called himself a "Jack-Mormon." He was raised in the Mormon Church but had fallen into apostasy in later years. He drank, chewed tobacco, and was known to use occasional, hearty bursts of profanity. He would be a cinch to turn to Christ. Suffice it to say that I got my butt handed to me on this one. Not only was he not my first convert, but I learned more about trying to proselytize him than I thought was possible even to know.

One thing about Mormons is that they dye their doctrine deep into the cerebral cortex. It is decidedly not gray matter… It is a Mormon matter. It didn't take long for us to agree not to discuss religion any further. ***What a bummer. I thought being a "missionary" was going to be easy.***

All four crews from the Intermountain Power Project converged upon the Holiday Inn in Craig, Colorado. Gale Chappell and Bob Daniels accompanied us for the kick-off. Gale put strict spending rules in place for our meals. It was only about half of the IRS guidelines. Gale was very tight with

IPSC money. His byline to us about expenses was simple. "You are supposed to stay nourished, not get fat!"

I was surprised that the Colorado Ute Electric Association allowed so many people to come into the Craig plant. Each of the Intermountain Shift Supervisors took their crew members and joined one of the shifts at the plant and rotated with them.

The Craig Plant was three 450 MW units and was equipped with B&W boilers and General Electric turbine and generators. Each unit was almost identical to the Holcomb or the Intermountain Plant, with the most significant difference being the size of the units. The Intermountain Plant had the largest drum boilers that B&W ever made. It was a huge plant. The single biggest difference in all the plants besides the size was the direct current (DC) tie between Intermountain and Los Angeles.

Craig Plant

Since the Shift Supervisor had no official duties at the Craig Plant other than training our crew members, we could go anywhere we wanted. It only took us a few days to realize that we could assign our people to work directly with the Colorado Ute operators in the daily execution of their duties, relieving the pressure of us specifically training them. The Craig personnel, for the most part, didn't mind because they would pawn off the dirty jobs to the Intermountain operators so they could get real-world experience. Everyone was happy... Almost everyone. The new Intermountain operators found that life as an auxiliary operator in a coal plant could be hot, dirty, hard work.

The first few days at Craig were interesting. However, each additional day started dragging longer and slower. I was heartsick and missing Vangie and the kids more each day. Intermountain would only pay for one long-distance telephone call home every other day for three minutes maximum. There were, of course, no cell phones in 1983.

The Holiday Inn began to feel like a prison without bars. Since we rotated with the crew we 'shadowed' at the plant, we shared their days off. I visited my family in Montrose on one of the weekends. It didn't help with my homesickness. I missed Vangie and the kids more than words could express.

We just started our graveyard shifts when Vangie left a message at the hotel. I got it when I arrived that morning to go to bed. It scared me. My first thought was something happened to her or one of the kids. I called back as soon as I received the message.

"Hello, Vangie speaking." I loved her voice, and just hearing it made me miss her even more.

"I just got the message that you called. Is everything okay?" I asked, trying not to sound frantic even though I was.

"Everything is fine. Neil Mecklenburg called and has an offer on the house for $82,500.00."

"Wow! That is better than I thought we would get." We listed the house for $84,900.00. I was prepared to take any offer greater than $81,500.00. "Does he think the people are good for it and can come up with the money?"

"He said they looked good on paper and had enough for the down payment." She paused. "They want possession as soon as possible as they are moving into Garden City from someplace else."

I thought for a moment before answering hesitantly. "Well, they still need to get a loan and do all the other stuff that goes with it. This is not a bad thing." I lowered my voice slightly and dropped into self-pity mode. "I miss you and the kids so bad I can't stand it. The sooner we can get back together, the better."

She didn't miss a chance to take a shot. "You were the one that wanted to do all of this, not me." The phone went silent for a few moments. I was angry and hurt and wanted to lash out, but she was absolutely right. I brought this on myself. I finished by talking to the kids for a few minutes. Hearing their voices made me ache.

The remaining graveyard shift drug by as always. I decided to surprise Vangie and the kids by coming to Garden City during the upcoming long change. My crew was going back to Delta and since I rode to Craig with Steve, I decided to take a Greyhound bus from Craig, Colorado all the way to Garden City.

I had never ridden a bus before because if I had, I would have never done it this time. What an out-of-control experience it turned out to be! Someone would have to put a loaded gun to my head and force me to ever ride one again. I would unquestionably hitchhike before I would step foot on another bus.

I had not been on the bus for more than an hour when a fight broke out in the back. The driver then kicked a couple of younger guys who appeared to be drunk off the bus. He used a baseball bat to enforce his disembark order. I thought passengers might have to intervene to help, but he was one tough dude. About a mile outside of Granby, Colorado the engine failed on the bus. We were stuck at the side of the road for several hours, waiting for another bus to rescue us.

I finally walked into Granby and finding a payphone, called Vangie asking if she would drive the five-hour trip to Denver and pick me up. I told her everything that happened just to get as far as Granby and that it would probably take all weekend to get to Garden City. She readily agreed and prepared to leave for Denver. Even though she had to pack and prepare herself and the kids for the trip, she still reached Denver about 30 minutes before I did.

Our reunion at Pat and Gloria's house was emotional. It was so nice to see her again. You don't realize how much you will miss someone until they are not around. The kids hugged me tightly and made me realize that this separation was not well thought out.

Once we were back home in Garden City, I signed the offer for the house and arranged for the moving company to pack and load based on the anticipated closing date Neil

Mecklenburg gave us. Intermountain would pay for the storage of our household goods for up to 6 months. This was good because the tenement apartment in Delta would only hold about a quarter of our stuff.

Don Unger caught me up on the latest at the Holcomb Plant. Turns out, I was the beginning of a sizable plant exodus. Roy Minor resigned and went to the D.B. Wilson Power Plant in Kentucky. Dan Coleman also resigned!

It seems my bizarre prank call to Bonanza Plant opened the door for him to interview. He must have had a good day and remained positive during the interview because they hired him as a Shift Supervisor. This was almost hard to believe. I had a good laugh when Don told me about him quitting. I still had no idea at that moment that Dan was *far* from being out of my life.

Bill Elfman resigned, and Curt decided not to replace him. Brad just moved up into his slot. Obviously, this was not a surprise to anyone. Porky Pig resigned, but Don had no idea where he was going. Neither of us could care less so long as we never had to work with him again. Also, Bob Ellington, the Plant Engineer, resigned and went back to Indiana.

Three of the original Shift Supervisors and three of the five management positions in the front office were vacated within a month of each other. All these departures left the south wall of the administration building almost vacant, and the unit wasn't even running yet. *Holcomb's issues continued to deteriorate.*

It was incredibly difficult to say goodbye to Vangie and the kids again. Unfortunately, I had to go back to Craig and finish my time there training the Intermountain operators.

The final days in Craig stand out as the longest, most lonely time I have ever spent on this planet. I was depressed to the point of despairing about life on more than one occasion. I kept asking myself, "God, what have I done?" Life seemed out of kilter. Nothing felt right. Everything seemed skewed towards the dark. There was an intense and painful emptiness within me that I had never experienced before.

While I tried to walk in some form of joy and not take things too seriously, I found myself increasingly moody and cold to my crew. I hated being away from Vangie and the kids. Plus, living in a Holiday Inn and eating at a small number of restaurants day-in and day-out was getting tedious. I was trapped like a hamster on a wheel that would not stop. It resembled a repeating nightmare.

Eventually, the last days at Craig slowly, painfully arrived. I was ecstatic as I flew from Hayden back to Garden City. I could hardly wait to see Vangie and the girls again.

It took a few days to pack and prepare for the move. Unfortunately, the closing date on the house was pushed back a couple of weeks due to the buyers being required to correct something on their credit report. This was a HUGE setback to me because I had timed everything around the anticipated closing date on the house. Plus, it left us worried that the sale might fall through. It didn't matter. I had to get back to the plant in Delta, and I certainly wouldn't leave without Vangie and the kids this time.

Neil Mecklenburg told us that we could close on the sale from Delta. The closing company in Garden City would simply send the papers to a closing company in Delta and we could just show up and sign the documents there. This was all I needed to hear. Our trek to Delta was now set in stone. *Oddly, this remote home closing played a stunningly important role in the adoption of our son almost two years later. Sometimes, the interconnections in our daily lives are God-directed and do not have any practical explanation.*

The movers arrived and professionally finished packing and loading our things on the truck. We pre-separated our household goods to allow most of them to be relegated to a storage facility in Salt Lake City, with the rest being delivered to Delta. When the final items were loaded, the doors on the truck slammed closed and they began their trek to Salt Lake City.

We made the rounds and said goodbye to everyone. Oddly, the most difficult goodbye was to Gordon and Lois Nelson. There is no question they already knew we were on the wrong path. However, they remained supportive to the end. Gordon told me that he was good friends with Bob Smith, the Senior Pastor at Valley Assembly of God in Salt Lake City. It was a large Church that made significant inroads in Salt Lake, the heart of the Mormon world. Gordon said that he called and told Bob all about us and our move to Delta.

We stayed the final night at the Hilton Inn in Garden City. We were exhausted from directing the movers, cleaning the house, and finishing the last-minute details. We enjoyed a nice relaxing dinner, took long showers, and retired to bed... Completely drained. Waking early the next morning we devoured breakfast and headed west on Highway 50, saying goodbye to Garden City for what we thought was the last time. *Funny how things can change.*

CHAPTER 7
A FORCED MEETING

The trip to Denver from Garden City was always slow because of an abundance of small towns, essentially speed traps, in western Kansas and eastern Colorado. After finally reaching Lamar, Colorado we turned northwest on Highway 287 through Eads, Kit Carson, Hugo, and then onto Limon, where we caught Interstate – 70 into Denver.

I was always amused by coming to Eads, Colorado. A large billboard on Highway – 287 said, *"Eads will meet your needs."* Eads was about 350 people. I think there was one restaurant, a filling station, a bar, and maybe a food store. If gas, junk food, and liquor were the sum of your needs, they could apparently fill the bill... Anything else? You apparently had to go back to Lamar or onto Limon. The trip from Lamar, Colorado to Limon on Highway – 287 was always monotonous and sleep-inducing.

We were making excellent time (translation; speeding) and had already blown through Eads and Kit Carson. The kids slept a good part of the trip, depleted from the previous day's activities. Things were smooth until we got about 20 or 30 miles outside of Hugo, Colorado. The speed limit was 55 MPH, and I was doing at least 65 MPH when the Saab engine quit running. It was exactly as if I shut the ignition key off. I tried fiddling with the accelerator, but the engine and car continued to quickly slow down until coming to a dead stop. At the very last moment, I pushed in on the clutch and coasted safely off the right side of the road.

"What's wrong?" Vangie asked, obviously freaked out as we coasted to a stop.

"It just quit running!" I exclaimed, trying to discern what could have happened.

We came to rest *directly* in front of a long driveway with a picturesque, older farmhouse off in the distance. It was probably about 150 yards or so to the house sitting on the end of that driveway. Most of Eastern Colorado is sparsely populated, tedious farmland. There were virtually no homes or structures of any sort for several miles prior to here, or after.

I tried starting the Saab. The engine cranked just fine. There didn't appear to be a battery or starter issue. It just would not start. We gassed up in Lamar, so I still had plenty of fuel showing on the gage. Vangie unloaded the kids while I opened the hood and looked for issues in the engine compartment. There was nothing abnormal that I could see. I had a small tool kit under the hatchback floor in the tiny storage area.

The car was packed to the gills as only Vangie could pack. I had to pull some stuff out and set it on the ground to reach the tool kit. There was virtually no traffic on Highway 287. I felt lucky that we stopped near a farmhouse.

As I unloaded the back of the car, Brandi told Vangie she had to go potty and Vangie also needed to use the bathroom. We decided to walk to the farmhouse and see if anyone was home. We herded the kids up the rutted, dirt lane to the farmhouse and knocked on the back door. The wear and attrition on the pathway suggested it was the main entrance to the aging farmhouse. It only took a few moments before the door slowly opened.

A woman in her mid to late 40s looked out the door. "Can I help you?" she asked apprehensively.

"Yes, my wife and two little girls and I just broke down in front of your driveway. I was wondering if we could use your bathroom and maybe borrow your phone to call for help?"

She looked over my shoulder at Vangie and the girls, carefully studying them before answering, "That would be fine. Please come in."

We entered directly into the poorly lit kitchen of the old farmhouse. There was a large dining table with a chair pulled out. A Bible was sitting open where the chair was pulled out.

"The bathroom is down that hall on the left." She pointed down a dimly lit hallway. The house was old but tidy. She was clean and well-dressed considering we were a million miles from nowhere in eastern Colorado.

I tended to Brittanie while Brandi and Vangie disappeared into the bathroom. The lady looked a little nervous as she said, "My husband is out in the field. I was just reading for a bit before starting lunch." I felt like she was making sure I knew someone else besides her was around.

Trying to break the ice and be conversive I answered her. "I understand. Looks like you are reading a good book."

She seemed a little embarrassed and gave me an odd look. "Yeah, I think so." She didn't seem very convinced that she was reading a good book. She then changed the subject. "What is wrong with your car?"

"I don't have a clue. It was running perfectly, and then it just quit with no warning. We left Garden City, Kansas after breakfast this morning, and everything was fine."

She raised her eyebrows. "Where are you headed?"

"We are moving from Garden City, Kansas to Delta, Utah. We planned to spend the night in Denver with my wife's sister and her husband."

We talked for a couple more minutes before Vangie and Brandi rambled back from the bathroom. Brandi was trying to take in the grainy pictures and wall decorations.

"Thank you so much for your hospitality!" Vangie exclaimed as she re-entered the kitchen and guided Brandi in front of her. "We were going to stop in the next town, but the car had other plans." They both laughed.

When it appeared they were okay together, I felt comfortable returning to the car and leaving Vangie and the kids at the farmhouse.

I looked at the lady and asked, "Would it be okay if my wife and girls stay here while I try to figure out what is wrong with the car?"

"That would be fine. I will be starting lunch for my husband in a bit. You and your family are welcome to have lunch with us."

"That's very nice of you. Hopefully, I can get the car running, and we can get out of your hair." I left the kitchen and returned to the Saab as quickly as possible. Everything I removed from the back of the car was sitting on the ground, and even though there was not much traffic, I didn't want anything stolen.

I worked for several years as a mechanic. I knew what items required checking to help determine what went wrong. I cracked open a fuel line to the fuel injection unit. 1979 Saab's used Bosch Mechanical Fuel Injection. This is a very simple system that runs with high fuel pressure. Therefore, if the fuel pump is running, it couldn't be vapor-locked. As soon as I turned the switch on and tried to start the car, the gas line that I loosened squirted gas over the top of the hood. Therefore, it had fuel.

I then pulled a spark plug wire off and fiddled around until I exposed the electrical connection. I put it near the grounded intake manifold and tried starting the car. Since the Saab hood opens forward and not backward, I could watch the engine as I tried to start it. It had a good, solid blue spark off the spark plug wire. Okay... *Fuel and spark.* These are the two essentials for an engine to run. Did the timing belt break? I was certain that Saab's are zero-tolerance engines. Had the timing belt broken at 60 MPH,, I would have heard the pistons crash into a non-moving valve train. However, when I cranked the engine, it sounded good. It seemed to have compression, and there were no abnormal sounds as I cranked it.

I put the spark plug wire back on and tried starting it. Nothing. It just cranked. I was stumped. It had fuel and spark, and the timing belt did not seem to be a problem. I then decided to pull a fuel injector out of the hole and test it for flow. Before now, I had just ensured there was fuel pressure *in* the Bosch fuel injection unit. If the fuel injection unit had a major malfunction, no fuel would be flowing to the fuel injectors.

Setting the fuel injector on the intake runners, I cranked the engine to start it. The fuel injector sprayed fuel as designed. I was beyond stumped. I didn't know where else to look. I decided to go back to the farmhouse and call my brother Mike. He owned a car dealership and was frequently at one of the Denver area dealer auto auctions. If he was there, he would most likely have the roll-bed truck that he used to transport vehicles back to his car lot in Grand Junction. I walked back to the farmhouse, thinking of what else I could check.

I knocked on the door. The lady answered with a smile on her face. She seemed more at ease now than she did earlier. "Ma'am, could I borrow your phone to make a collect call?"

She smiled and said, "Please call me Kate, and yes, you may use the phone." She pointed to the wall phone next to the hall in the kitchen. It was obvious she and Vangie were getting along very well. She seemed cheerful and relaxed now.

I called Mike. I explained everything that happened and everything I had done to this point. Mike was an amazing mechanic, and I implicitly trusted his car sense. I was hoping he could shed some light on our situation. He wasn't in Denver but said he would come with his roll bed truck if I couldn't get the car running.

Denver was about 4 hours away from Grand Junction. We were sitting about 2 or more hours from Denver. If he had to come and get us, it would have been a very, very long day. He told me to remove a spark plug and see if I could tell whether there was compression or not. Like me, he was struggling to understand that it had fuel and spark, yet the car wouldn't start. Since the kids were playing and Vangie seemed to be getting along well with Kate, I walked back to the Saab.

I wasn't sure if I had a spark plug socket or not. I dug into the poorly arranged tool kit but couldn't find a spark plug socket. This wasn't good. I walked back to the driver's side of the car, opened the door, and sat down in the driver's seat to think for a moment.

While thinking about what else to do, I casually reached the floor (Saab ignition keys were on the floor between the front seats) and tried to start the engine again. It started *IMMEDIATELY*. There was no hesitation and no issues whatsoever. It started as if nothing had ever been a problem. I couldn't believe it. I revved the engine several times, and it sounded fine. I let it run for a few minutes before shutting it off. I restarted it again, and it restarted IMMEDIATELY, sounding perfectly normal.

I was more stumped now than ever. I painstakingly loaded everything into the back of the car and slowly drove down the deeply rutted driveway to the farmhouse.

Vangie and Kate apparently heard the car come up near the back door, and they stepped out of the house as I exited the car. "What was wrong with it?" Vangie asked with a puzzled look on her face.

"I don't have a clue," I answered with an equally puzzled look. "I didn't change or fix anything. It just started. I have no idea why it quit and no idea why it started again." I paused for a moment and then looked directly at Vangie. "Maybe it is time for the Saab to go away?"

"Maybe." She answered, slightly shaking her head in agreement. I slipped into the house and called Mike, telling him what happened and that he, thankfully, wasn't needed. We then said goodbye to our gracious host. Kate hugged Vangie and the kids, and we were back on our way.

"Did you enjoy your visit with Kate?" I asked anxiously as we turned back onto Highway 287 from the driveway.

"It was okay." Vangie paused for a moment. "She accepted the Lord at Church last Sunday." She didn't elaborate. Typical of Vangie, she said all she was going to say.

"Don't leave me hanging!" I exclaimed. "What did you guys discuss?" I looked over at Vangie pleadingly.

She looked at me emotionless. "We just discussed Church and God."

"That's all you're going to say? What did you tell her?" I was excited and waiting to hear amazing things.

"I don't know." Vangie's voice was becoming irritated. "We discussed God and Church and the kids and a little bit of everything."

I was about to scream. It was apparent to me that the Saab stopped right at their driveway for a reason beyond an engine malfunction. I wanted to hear ALL the amazing details. I wanted to hear how Vangie dramatically led this woman to the Lord while the heavens opened and choirs of angels sang.

True to Vangie's character, she was satisfied with what she told me. As much as I wanted to hear the details of what happened, Vangie just sat in the passenger seat with the quiet dignity that I always loved... And, sometimes, really hated it.

Several minutes later, she looked at me and quietly said, "We were supposed to stop there."

That was it—no additional details. However, knowing Vangie as I did, her statement, "We were supposed to stop there," fully answered my questions. While I would have killed for the itty-bitty details, I knew I had heard everything I was going to hear and that it was all good.

The remainder of the trip to Delta was uneventful. We stopped and visited Pat and Gloria, staying the night in Denver, and then left early the next morning for the 10-hour completion of our journey. We rolled into Delta at dusk and went straight to the apartment. Vangie hadn't seen the apartment yet. She was wholly underwhelmed but took it in stride.

The moving truck arrived a few days late. We were sleeping on the floor of the tenement apartment, so it was nice to get some beds and additional clothes. Living out of a suitcase with two children was less than ideal. Anyway... *Woo Hoo! We were now officially residents of Delta, Utah or so I thought.*

CHAPTER 8
TO HELL AND BACK

Delta, Utah was a town centered around the Mormon Church. Any activities were conducted by or interconnected to the Church. There were only a couple of locally owned restaurants, so it was necessary to drive a significant distance to get to a chain restaurant of any sort. There were a couple of small grocery stores and a hardware store. Very little else was there.

In 1983, if you wanted a house in Delta, Utah you found a vacant lot and hired a builder. We started looking almost immediately and found a builder who would sell the lot and build the house you chose. We tentatively chose a lot and picked out a home. It was to be a three-bedroom, split-level style house. Looking for a home was exciting, but nothing else in Delta brought any excitement whatsoever.

Our first Sunday took us to the Valley Assembly of God in Salt Lake City. I made the huge mistake of calling Bob Smith, the Senior Pastor of the Church. I used the information provided by Gordon and Lois Nelson. Gordon had, indeed, called him and told him about us. He invited us to stay in their visiting missionary quarters in an on-site suite at the Church Campus. Why was it a mistake to call him?

I was so far out of my league and unprepared that I did not comprehend what I was even saying when I told people we were going to be missionaries to the Mormon Church. The old saying, "When you are too ignorant to know how ignorant you are, you are *way* too ignorant", certainly applied here.

The visit to Valley Assembly just pumped me up and prolonged the inevitable. We were no more prepared to take on the Mormon Church than we were prepared to set up a clinic and do brain surgery.

That Sunday we were guests of honor at this huge Assembly of God Church in Salt Lake City. They had Vangie and I stand up in the service, and the Church membership prayed for us. We went to lunch with Bob and several of the Church Pastors. They were pleased that we had made the decision to do what we were doing, but they also warned us how difficult it would be to make any inroads whatsoever. They said the biggest problem we would face would be discouragement.

I had no idea at the time just how true their words were. We were stepping into a situation in which we were wholly unprepared. After finishing Church and lunch, we returned to the "mission field" (Delta), feeling quite energized with our new anointing.

Regardless of how bad Delta was, the Intermountain Power Plant was one of the nicest in the United States. Los Angeles Department of Water and Power was spending money on this place like there was no tomorrow.

The plant management implemented a Responsibility, Goal, and Objective (RGO) merit-based pay system. You were required to establish your written goals and objectives while taking on certain responsibilities.

This model of management was designed to develop subject matter experts (SMEs). You did what every shift supervisor in every plant did, but you were also assigned systems or areas of the plant, and you alone were the chief decision maker for that system or equipment. I was intrigued by this system and enjoyed the complexity of this plant.

Back in Delta, Vangie and the kids were miserable. Pure and simple, *we were outsiders*. We would always be outsiders until we decided to be Mormons. There was nothing to do in that little, depressing town and the kids were bored and driving Vangie crazy.

The tenement apartment building was built cheaper than the mobile homes in Rock Springs. Our neighbors directly above us procreated like rabbits almost every single night. Their bed frame squeaked violently, the floor shook, and we heard any other sounds that might accompany this experience. It was uncomfortably awkward and gave way to total annoyance as time passed.

Valley Assembly of God was too far away to attend every Sunday. It was over two and a half hours one way. We settled on an Assembly of God Church in Santaquin, Utah. It was a bit over an hour from Delta and was a small, desperate group of Christians that met in an aging, dilapidated, former Mormon Church that had to be well over a hundred years old. If you were in a good mood when you arrived, you would be depressed when you left. If you were in a depressed mood when you arrived, you fit right in. Because of the distance from Delta and the fact that we were still outsiders we did not get involved with anything at that Church.

There you have it. 'Missionary' life in a nutshell. We were no more missionaries than we were 'called' to be there. Could we have made it work? Of course! Had we been mature, CALLED (by God, not by my blind ambitions), prepared, and equipped. Unfortunately, this is like saying I would be a millionaire if I just had a million dollars. We found ourselves calling and talking to Pastor and Lois Nelson on a regular basis.

There was no question that the Church situation in Garden City was getting worse. Virginia Stratton took sick and died. She was one of the pillars of that Church. John, her husband, was the workhorse behind the bus ministry. He also kept the Royal Rangers program running.

Royal Rangers was almost identical to Boy Scouts but organized and administered through the Assembly of God Church. He was grieving the loss of his wife of 50 years and the Nelsons feared he could not continue doing all his duties at Church. They didn't know who would pick them up if he stopped.

Gordon and Lois Nelson also commiserated that the strife that was plaguing them before we left was getting worse, much worse. They were not doing well and wished we had not moved to Delta. They told us there were very few families left in the Church that they trusted. You could tell they were experiencing tremendous stress, and it was getting worse by the day.

Our house on Arapaho Street finally closed after the buyers dealt with several issues. Neil Mecklenburg and the title company in Garden City sent all the papers to a title company in Delta. Yes, they had ONE title company in Delta. We blindly signed the papers, trusting the realtor and title company agents and deposited the check after closing. We had no idea that there was an error in the closing papers that would not be found until 18 months later. In fact, this ended up being one of the most incredible miracles that we have ever experienced.

We had now been in Delta for about 8 weeks as a family and we were miserable. One evening we went to look at the house we were building. It was about the only 'family activity' we had in that raunchy little town. The contractor finished the foundation work, and a good part of the initial framing was now complete. We walked into it that evening and ventured through the wooden skeleton where the rooms would eventually be. *There was no excitement.* There was nothing. As we looked through the skeletal structure of what was supposed to be our brand-new future home, I peered into Vangie's golden eyes and saw she was just going through the motions. I realized at that moment we were both completely disheartened. Nothing felt like home. *Nothing felt right.*

Earlier that day there was a birthday party for a little girl that Brandi knew in our tenement. She was the same age as Brandi. All the kids in the apartment complex were invited except Brandi. I knew this hurt Vangie terribly. She didn't say much, but I could see it in her eyes. Brandi was as cute as could be and had a very dark complexion. We didn't know if it was her complexion or the fact that we weren't Mormons that caused her not to be invited. We highly suspected the latter.

As we looked through the partially framed house, I touched Vangie's arm and said, "I really screwed up, didn't I?"

"What are you talking about?" She replied in a puzzled voice.

"Moving us here. This was such a mistake, wasn't it?" I looked more to see her reaction than what she would say. Her body language confirmed it even though her words didn't.

"We're here... what difference does it make now?" This was a classic Vangie answer. Her attitude was simple: *why look back? Just make the best of things and move forward.* She wasn't going to engage even though I could tell every fiber of her being detested this place.

We finished looking at the house and went home, putting the kids to bed. Our nightly xxx serenade from the apartment above was on-time and relentless. We couldn't catch a break. As I lay in bed trying to tune out the ruckus above us, I knew I had to do something. We would never make it here.

The next morning at the plant I called Holcomb Station and asked to speak to Brad Schultz. I was immediately connected.

"Brad, Mark Gregg here. How are you doing?"

"Good. I didn't expect to hear from you. What's going on?"

"Things aren't working out as I planned here. The plant is fine. There are no issues there, but Delta is a Mormon enclave, and we are outsiders. I don't think we will ever fit in here and my wife is seriously not happy." I was being a total weasel, but I didn't want this to fail. I continued by bluntly asking him, "would you consider hiring me back?"

There were several moments of silence. It seemed like an eternity. "We don't have an opening for a Shift Supervisor. I think we would take you back in a heartbeat as a Control Room Operator."

"Done!" I started laughing to diffuse my embarrassment. Crawling back to your former employer was a new one for me and I felt naked on a busy street corner with everyone staring at me.

"Seriously, are you interested in coming back as a Control Operator?" Brad seemed sincere and not condescending in any way. This was a good sign.

"Brad, I have invested almost 10 years in my marriage and have two children. I don't want to sacrifice this for a powerplant. Vangie loved Garden City and we had a lot of friends there. I would come back as a Control Room Operator in a heartbeat. Frankly, it was the best job I ever had." I was ashamed of myself and felt like a total loser and snake for using Vangie as the entire excuse for returning. I just didn't want to tip my hat that *I was a complete idiot.*

"Let me talk to Curt. Can I call you back?"

"Of course. I am at the plant today. I can call you back later or you can call me at home tonight." I paused. "Let me give you my home phone number."

"That works. I will talk to Curt and get back to you."

I gave him our home phone number and thanked him. I was so glad the call was over. It was a horribly difficult call to make but it finally felt like I was doing something right for a change.

The remainder of the day bled by slowly. I was in rapt anticipation of a return call from Brad. I was terrified the call wouldn't come. Arriving home that afternoon, I asked Vangie if there had been any calls. I had no more than asked her this when the phone rang. I jumped and grabbed it before she could.

"Hello, Mark Gregg here."

"Mark, it's Brad. You have a minute?"

"You bet. What did you find out?"

"It's a go if you want to come back as a Control Room Operator. You already know what it pays, and we will pay for your move, house hunting trip, and all moving expenses including the $2,000.00 moving bonus." I was blown away that they would move us and still pay the moving bonus exactly as if I had never worked there before.

"That's fantastic!" I said, trying to control my emotions.

"If you want to move on this, I will have Gloria call you tomorrow."

"Absolutely, this is a go. When do you want me to start?"

"We are getting deep into the start-up. As far as I am concerned the sooner, the better!" He was very upbeat and it thrilled me that the door was being opened so widely.

I hung up the phone and looked at Vangie who was looking at me with total confusion on her face. "How would you like to leave this place and move back to Garden City?" I was trying to contain my excitement as I spoke.

"How is that even possible?" she asked incredulously.

"I am going back as a Control Room Operator. They are paying all our moving expenses, house hunting trips, and even the $2,000.00 bonus for moving. Can you believe it?"

"Wait a minute." She paused with an irritated look of concern on her face. "You took a Control Room Operator's job?" I was shocked at the angry tone in her voice. "That's an hourly job and pays less than you were making as a Shift Supervisor."

"Yes, but they are in full-blown start-up now and there will be tons of overtime. I will unquestionably make more as a Control Room Operator than I would as a Shift Supervisor. Plus, the first Shift Supervisor opening would be mine." Brad never said this, but I needed Vangie's acceptance right now. I thought I did the right thing and yet she was acting like I screwed-up royally.

"I hope you know what you are doing. I can't believe you are returning to a place you hated." Her anger became more pronounced as she spoke.

"I didn't hate it. I just thought we were supposed to come here." A moment that I felt would be happy or exciting for both of us had put Vangie squarely in attack mode.

"Oh, right… You didn't hate it." She turned condescending and sarcastic. "You tell yourself whatever it takes to make this right in your eyes." She paused, and her voice turned menacing. "Do you ever listen to yourself and how ridiculous you sound when you are trying to justify something?"

I was so pissed that I thought I would burst a blood vessel in my brain. Here I thought I was doing something right for a change, and now… *This was stupid, and I was stupid. Garden City was stupid, moving was stupid, and she was fighting mad.*

I stormed out the front door slamming it as HARD as possible and kept walking. I began praying under my breath for help. I was so depressed, so angry, and so confused that I needed something or someone to tell me things would be okay.

I walked until I cooled down and could come back and be civil. When I walked back into the apartment, Vangie's face and body language made it clear to me that she was still upset. "Listen," I said slowly and calmly, "I know that coming here was a mistake. We both know it. This is a chance to go back and make things right."

"Fine." She looked at me with fire in her eyes. "We can go back, but I better not *EVER* hear you complain about the plant or that you are a Control Room Operator. You need to think very carefully about why you left there in the first place!"

My anger again exploded but I somehow managed to keep it under wraps. "I will be extremely careful. You will never hear me complain about my job or anything else when we return."

"When is all this taking place?" she asked with resignation in her voice.

"Right away. They want me back in Holcomb as soon as possible, so I will give Bob Daniels the option of a two-week notice. With no more than what is happening at the plant, he will probably just tell me to hit the road."

We discussed the situation some more. Even though she detested living in Delta, I could not get her to openly admit that this was a good idea. I decided to call in sick the next day and work out the details of returning to Garden City with Gloria and make sure there were no 'hitches' with us returning to Sunflower.

The following day proved that everything was a go-to return to Garden City. Gloria told me that as soon as I could break away from here, we could do a house-hunting trip. I knew I must tell Bob what was happening so I could determine when to do the house-hunting trip, schedule the movers, and get the ball rolling.

The next day, I told Bob what was happening. I used Vangie as the culprit again. I know... *What a stinking, cowardly thing to do, right?* However, there was no other way to explain my sudden desire to leave. What was I supposed to do? Tell them the truth... ***That I was a total idiot, and they were fools for hiring me in the first place?***

Bob surprised me. He asked if I would go for a ride with him. I accepted, and we drove around for about two long, long, long hours. He wanted to know if Vangie and I would consider counseling. He felt very strongly it was a mistake for me to leave. He launched into a spiel about how good my future was at Intermountain. At one point, with no direct connection to what he was saying, I asked him, "Bob, are you Mormon?" I could tell it stunned him because his face turned red.

He completely stopped talking for a moment, squinted, and then looked at me (while driving) and said, "I don't think that's any of your business and certainly not appropriate for this conversation." *So... He obviously isn't a Mormon.* I am certain he would have immediately and proudly said "yes" if he was.

It took him a few minutes to get back onto his pitch as to why I should stay at Intermountain. When it was all said and done, he told me that if Vangie and I would not consider counseling and if I was steadfast in my quest to leave, he would arrange for the paperwork. I told him I would get back to him.

We were still under contract for our home that was being built. I went to the contractor and told him we were leaving Delta and asked if we could back out of the deal due to leaving the area. We had paid $1,000.00 earnest money to get the home-building process started.

We were in a new subdivision, the only new one in Delta, and the demand far exceeded the development rate. He agreed to release us from the contract and just put the house up for sale if we would forfeit $500.00. Remember, this was 1983. That was still a lot of money. However, I agreed to it because we were under contract and this seemed to be the least messy way out of it.

We did our house-hunting trip in Garden City early the next week. After meeting with Neil Mecklenburg, we began looking at houses. We found several homes in our price range, but nothing really excited us. We were staying at the Hilton Inn during the house-hunting trip. Several of the Holcomb plant personnel knew we were back in town, including Brad, Curt, and Don Unger.

The second day of unsuccessful house hunting was disappointing but not unexpected. We arrived back at the Hilton at about 6:00 PM. The message light was flashing on the telephone in our room. It was a message to call Dan Coleman at our earliest convenience. The area code was 801. I recognized immediately that this was Utah. Why would Dan Coleman want to talk to me? *We hated each other.*

I called his number, and Dan immediately answered the phone. Remember my call to Stan Gordan pretending to be Dan? Apparently, Dan followed up, interviewed at Bonanza Plant, was hired, and was now living in Vernal, Utah. His former Control Room Operator at the Holcomb Plant told him we were back in town looking for a new house in Garden City.

He went into incredible detail about how badly he would like to forego paying a realtor and sell his house directly to us. He assured me he would make us a killer deal on it. He left a key with Bill Winchester, his next-door neighbor and an Auxiliary Operator at the Holcomb Plant. I told Dan we would look at his place the next morning.

Bill Winchester's wife let us into Dan's house the next morning. We, of course, did not say anything to Neil Mecklenburg. I just told him we needed to start house hunting later that morning. After a full walk-thru, we didn't care for Dan's house very much because the basement wasn't finished and it only had one bathroom. It did have a two-car garage and was certainly in our price range, but other than this, we were ambivalent.

That afternoon Neil took us to see several more houses. They were either too expensive, or we didn't care for them. Dan's house was looking better all the time. Back at the Hilton, I called Dan's room that evening.

"Dan Coleman." He answered curtly.

"Dan, Mark Gregg here. Julie Winchester let us into your house this morning. We did a thorough walk thru." I paused intentionally to irritate him a bit. "We aren't sure it will work for us. We need an extra bedroom and bathroom and aren't fully in love with the floor plan."

"Tell you what…" He cleared his throat. "We put a lot of money down on that house and we need it back because we found one here in Vernal that we really like." He paused again. "What if I were to drop the price another $2,000.00, and then after you get your loan and close, I would rebate you another $1,000.00 to spend on a bedroom and bathroom in the basement?" I was shocked. This was a steal on that house even if we didn't care for it much. We could finish the basement very nicely and have a much nicer house than the one on Arapaho Street for about the same money. I was impressed with the deal he was offering. His house was only two years old and in great shape.

"Dan, let me talk to Vangie and call you back."

We hung up, and I put the full-court press on Vangie for Dan's house. We both recognized the shortcomings in the house but also knew we had not found anything in our price range that was to our liking. She was as surprised and pleased as I was with Dan's new price as well as the rebate he was giving back to finish the basement. There was one small problem. I didn't trust Dan.

I called Neil Mecklenburg and explained the situation, and asked if he would handle the contract and closure. He agreed to do everything for 1.5% of the selling price. I then called Dan back and told him we would buy his house if he split Neil's fee to handle the contract and closure.

This time, he had to call me back. It only took him about 5 minutes. *We now had a deal*. Wow! We just purchased Dan Coleman's house. I couldn't believe it. *Oddly enough, I still wasn't done dealing with Dan Coleman… Not even close.*

Dan apparently bought the house he wanted in Vernal and moved his furniture out a week later. Neil handled the contract and closing for us to purchase Dan's house. We scheduled the movers to pick up our household goods at the Delta apartment and from the Salt Lake City storage. They packed and gathered our goods and moved them into 2015 Mohawk Street. Three weeks after calling Brad about returning, I started work at Holcomb Station. The plant was deeply embedded in the start-up and things weren't progressing well, but I was back. Life has many odd twists and turns. The entire Delta ordeal was certainly one of them.

CHAPTER 9
BACKWARD ISN'T FORWARD

Returning to the plant revealed the massive problems taking place daily in what was rapidly becoming a train wreck versus a power plant start-up. I am certain this contributed to their willingness to bring me back. The plant had slipped further behind schedule and was required to make first energy by a specific date or lose a substantial amount of REA funding.

To generate electricity by the drop-dead date they attempted to roll the turbine and synchronize the generator before anything was ready. Due to multiple bad decisions, they mortally damaged the main generator and failed miserably in their attempt to make initial energy. This caused a serious domino effect on plant financing and REA loans. They were almost forced to cancel the plant, but it was so close to completion that outside financing was brought into the project to keep it viable.

To say it was awkward coming back to the Holcomb Plant as a Control Room Operator is a massive understatement. It could have worked okay, other than the whole maturity thing that I hadn't mastered yet.

One of the first things I did to prop up my bruised ego upon returning as a Control Room Operator was to write dozens of sticky notes and paste them on the control board near different switches, buttons, and controllers. I decided that the existing control room operators were very ignorant, and I would help educate them. Most of the sticky notes contained good information. However, they were not received as well as I would have liked.

Not surprisingly, many people saw the sticky notes as a personal affront from an egomaniac Control Operator who was now the low man on the seniority totem pole. Unfortunately, I still viewed myself as a senior shift supervisor and a very knowledgeable one. This could have blown up in my face far worse than it did had it not been for the fact that we were deep into the start-up and mistakes were being made continuously by everyone on almost a daily basis. This meant the plant staff didn't have as much time to discuss and exaggerate issues like this one.

Other than the initial offense with the sticky notes, I managed to keep myself out of trouble and remained a control operator for a short period of time. When the generator repair was finally complete, we successfully started the plant. It was much easier this time because construction crews had a chance to complete more instrumentation and system check-outs during the extensive generator repair.

As the only control room operator with actual plant operational experience, I was extremely comfortable during the start-up period while enjoying the start-up immensely from the control room. I was only a Control Operator for a few weeks after we finally synchronized the generator to the grid.

Another Shift Supervisor left unexpectedly, creating an opening in the Shift Supervisor ranks. I was immediately promoted. My entire time as a Control Operator was less than two months. While I thoroughly enjoyed being in the control room, I was also pleased to be back in the shift supervisor's office.

The Shift Supervisors were paired during the initial weeks of online operation. This allowed for two Shift Supervisors on a shift instead of one. This was because the Joy-Niro dry atomized scrubber presented formidable challenges in the start-up phase, requiring almost full-time supervision. This was the first dry atomized scrubber in the United States and no one had operational experience with this technology.

The Niro atomizers spun at over 10,000 RPM and created a semi-dry spray of limestone slurry that hyper-mixed with the flue gas stream, neutralizing the acids in the furnace exhaust. This stream of neutralized ash was then removed in the fabric filter (bag house) and disposed of in the landfill. Every time an upset occurred, the entire absorber vessel would turn into a massive block of concrete requiring crews to dynamite it out. It was an incredible mess!

I was paired with John Russock. He was the oldest Shift Supervisor, and I was still the youngest and unquestionably the most immature. John was easygoing, unshakeable, and more than happy to allow me to run unchecked. I loved the start-up phase, which usually found me going to the scrubber, back to the control room, and at least three other places before he even finished doing shift turnover.

His daily mode was to arrive, participate in shift turnover and then go down to the administration building for his daily 'constitutional.' He would always take a newspaper to read while he sat on the throne, waiting for his body to respond. Personally, I didn't care what he did. While he was on the toilet in the admin building, I discussed the plant operation with the control room operator(s) and attended to any pressing issues.

One day, on what started as a normal afternoon shift, John grabbed a newspaper and nodded to me that he was initiating his daily routine as he left the control room. Unfortunately, the unit tripped about 15 minutes after he left, and we lost all station service. This is called a 'black plant'. The only things left running are some of the emergency lighting and a few DC oil pumps. All the equipment, pumps, and systems immediately shut down and left us with safety valves screaming as they relieved the over-pressured boiler, steam lines hammering and slamming against their hangers from the severe water hammer. Most of the operators were scared-silly due to their inexperience in these situations.

About 30 seconds after the power was lost amidst the instant chaos that ensues in a large plant like this, the radio burst forth. "Need an ambulance in the admin building! I repeat, need an ambulance in the admin building!" The voice was John Russock, and he sounded terrified. This was scary because he was always so low-key. I immediately hollered at my Control Room Operator to use the outside line (a phone line that did not go through the plant switchboard) and get an ambulance coming.

I just finished telling the operator to get an ambulance dispatched when the radio again cracked, "Cancel the ambulance! Cancel the ambulance! I repeat, cancel the ambulance! There is no need for the ambulance in the admin building!"

I immediately grabbed the control room radio microphone. "John, are you okay?" I could not fathom what prompted his cry for an ambulance and then the almost instant reversal.

"Everything is fine. We don't need an ambulance! Tend to the unit!" His voice was more animated than usual, but he seemed certain that everything was okay. I took him at his word and started working towards a safe shutdown on the floundering plant.

It took about 20 minutes to get a major circuit breaker reclosed in the switchyard to return power back into the plant auxiliary systems. From there, it took about 30 more minutes to get the necessary pumps and equipment running to quell the over-temperature alarms and tame the extreme water hammers we were experiencing. Black plant situations could be stress-paralyzing, but I had been through so many that I didn't freak out as I once did, and as many on the shift did that evening.

About an hour after things settled down and we were working towards an eventual restart, John walked into the control room with his head suspiciously low and went straight to the Shift Supervisors office. I followed him there as he sat down.

"What the heck happened down there that you called for an ambulance?" I asked excitedly. "You scared the crap out of us!"

John looked at me with an expression of shame, guilt, and exasperation on his face before slowly iterating. "I was sitting on the toilet reading the newspaper. I was pushing with my eyes closed to finish the job when I heard an odd popping sound!" He then looked at me wild-eyed and shaking his head in disbelief. "I opened my eyes and was completely stone-blind! I thought I strained so hard that I snapped my optical nerve!" He paused when I couldn't contain myself and burst out laughing.

He shook his head slowly and continued. "I think it must have been the ballast in the fluorescent lights that made the popping sound. After the emergency lighting came on, I realized I wasn't blind and cancelled the ambulance."

By then, I was laughing so hard that my ribs were tearing loose from their tendons. I knew he wasn't joking by his expression and the rattled look on his face. I laughed until I could see he was getting seriously annoyed. I then went back to the control room and, out of respect for John, waited at least five minutes before I told the rest of the crew what happened.

John kept a low profile that night, leaving the restart of the main unit to me. He quietly slipped out to the scrubber to see what was happening there. Frankly, it was nice finding a bit of humor in an otherwise bad situation.

The next major issue happened a week later. The Holcomb Station uses two steam-driven boiler feed pumps and a small, 120,000 Lb/hr auxiliary boiler for start-up steam to the unit.

The 120,000 Lb/Hr auxiliary boiler was gas-fired and sat on the bottom floor in the northwest corner of the main boiler building. Like so many things at Holcomb, the control system on the auxiliary boiler was flawed. The operations group had written many work requests for the aux boiler because the forced draft fan control was poorly designed, and the linkage to the powerful fan would bind and lock.

That afternoon we were in the middle of a start-up trying to bring the main boiler up. The auxiliary boiler was currently supplying the building heat along with the large amount of steam necessary to run one of the steam-driven boiler feed pumps for the main boiler. As with most of the early start-ups, everything in the plant was fighting us. The main boiler drum level was swinging wildly as we tried to stabilize the plant to get the turbine load high enough so the boiler feed pump turbines could get their steam supply from their normal source, a steam extraction from the main turbine.

I was in the control room, and Curt and Brad were both observing, pretending to help. We had two control room operators working together. One of them focused on the steam drum level because it was so active and erratic due to steam flow and firing rate changes. I watched as the drum level in the boiler went low, and the operator rapidly increased the motive steam to the boiler feed pump turbine to catch the falling level.

At that moment, the linkage apparently bound and locked on the auxiliary boiler forced draft. As the steam pressure fell, the gas valve to the auxiliary boiler opened wide to increase the firing rate and bring the pressure back to its 150-psig setpoint. With full fuel flow and minimal air, the auxiliary boiler went completely fuel-rich!

Without warning a DEAFENING EXPLOSION violently shook the entire plant. The floor of the control room felt like it jumped several inches. Dozens of alarms sounded as dust from the drop-ceiling panels filled the control room adding to the fear and drama of the moment. I froze for a moment not knowing what to think or do. I tried to stay calm and maintain my composure.

A few moments later, one of the floor operators keyed his radio. "HOLY SHIT!!! THERE WAS A HUGE EXPLOSION DOWN HERE!!! I THINK IT WAS THE AUXILIARY BOILER!" He sounded panicked and out of breath.

I grabbed my hard hat and charged out of the control room. I didn't wait for the elevator but bounded the three floors to the basement, sliding my hands down the handrails while my feet hit every third or fourth step. The smoke and dust had fully filled the plant like a thick, acrid blanket.

Once I reached the bottom floor, I was coughing from the debris filling the air and my lungs. Approaching the auxiliary boiler, it became quite apparent it had exploded. The sides of the boiler were bowed out a couple of feet. What used to be a semi-rectangular structure was quite amusingly round. On the far end of the auxiliary boiler, there was a sight glass to do flame checks. This had blown completely off and blew through the wall like a projectile out of a cannon. The entire front end of the boiler blew completely off, bending large I-beams and support steel.

Thank God there was no lingering fire. The gas valves had tripped closed during or after the explosion, but there was still a fair amount of heat still in the area. It wasn't too much to handle but enough to make you slow down and approach cautiously. The oddest part of the explosion was the fact that there was absolutely no steam leakage! It was entirely a fire-side explosion.

Like the main boiler, the auxiliary boiler is primarily made up of 2.25" tubes filled with a water/steam mixture, with the fire being inside the large firebox formed by the tubes. Even with the massive deformation of the boiler casing, not one single tube of the 1000+ tubes leaked in the waterwalls or the superheater. I will never forget this strange anomaly.

To this day, the auxiliary boiler still operates with the sides puffed out from the explosion. It was impossible to pull

126

everything back into its original shape, so the construction crews just repaired the casing leaks, the I-beam, and other damage but left the auxiliary boiler with convex exterior walls. I nicknamed the auxiliary boiler "the pregnant pig."

It took the construction crews over a couple of weeks to repair the damage to the auxiliary boiler. The plant sat idle during this time. However, it was time well spent trying to get other systems and equipment finished or tested.

It was only a few more weeks before the Shift Supervisors stopped double shifting. John was a good, semi-silent partner, and we got along well together. In hindsight, he was a stabilizing influence on me. My knowledge of the plant was not nearly as good as I thought it was at the time, but it was still far ahead of my maturity level. John helped keep me in check.

CHAPTER 10
JESSICA

Things at the plant, though problematic, were simple compared to the trauma of returning to our previous lives in Garden City. Church wasn't the same. In the short time we were in Delta the atmosphere morphed from an enjoyable, loving fellowship to a dark, inflamed environment that felt more like an angry, two-party political caucus than it did a Church. Gone were the warm smiles and welcoming attitudes that were the hallmark of this Church. It was difficult to go to the Church now that most parishioners would sit in the pew with their arms crossed and a look of anger plastered on their faces.

Our return from Delta was not the happy homecoming of wayward prodigals I hoped it would be. Immediately upon returning to Garden City, Pastor Nelson provided us with keys to the Church and asked if we would resume as the Youth Leaders for the Youth Group. He had been semi-forced to put Terry and Brenda back in charge, a decision he was not happy with.

Pastor's decision to return the Youth Group to us caused an immediate rift between Terry and me. This strained our previously good friendship. Dwayne and Rene Stiles always sided with Terry and Brenda, which also cast a pall on our past friendship with them. They would now physically avoid being near us. Knowing they were upset with us was painful and difficult.

The Nelsons looked old and haggard. Their situation was deteriorating rapidly. They were receiving anonymous hate mail supposedly from 'random' parishioners, saying they should "resign for the good of the Church." Their crime? As far as I could tell, it was not allowing the Elgins and their family to run every aspect of the Church.

Our departure and time away from Garden City opened our eyes to the insidious effect that our previous alliance with the Elgins and Stiles had on us. Much like bind-weed curls around and chokes a healthy plant, we had been slowly manipulated away from the truth of the situation. If there was a silver lining to the Delta disaster, it was our realignment to the truth of what was happening at the Church in Garden City.

The Youth Group wasn't the same, either. They were restless and difficult to reach. These were the kids that prior to our leaving had opened their lives to us. They were now distant and even angry without any discernible reason. Our efforts to rally them fell flat, and attendance dwindled. We rapidly grew to over 80 kids before leaving. We were lucky now to have 20 kids show up, half of them late and cynical. It did not matter what we did. Things were dark and troubled. I began to blame myself for leaving and letting them, myself, and God down.

I would go straight to the Church in the mornings after finishing graveyard shifts. The Church would be vacant, and I would go to the altar, falling on my face, weeping, and praying. Most of the time I was begging the Lord to forgive me for my epic Delta, Utah failure.

Even though I understood in my mind the Christian precept of total forgiveness by the Blood of Christ, my heart could not break away from the ridiculous train wreck I caused by running off to Utah thinking I was some kind of proselytizing rock star and was going to enlighten and convert the entire Mormon Church to 'true' Christianity. *I was wrong on every possible level.*

I made a total fool of myself, a wreck of my family, and let down everyone we were close to in Garden City. Because of this, I fell into a pseudo-existence portraying a cheerful, full of faith, happy person on the outside, all the while *dying* on the inside. I was so depressed I could hardly lift my head, but I somehow managed to keep the façade that I was blissful and collected on the outside.

Frankly, this charade became more exhausting than shiftwork. After a few weeks of travail at the altar due to my abject failure, I began to realize I should use my time in prayer to ask for healing in the Church and not forgiveness for something that I had already been forgiven. It was difficult, but something I knew I must do. I slowly converted to focusing on the latter and not the former.

The bus ministry continued but was part of the tension in the Church. The Elgins wanted the buses to focus on kids from more "prominent" neighborhoods and not the Vietnamese and Hispanic trailer parks which I felt was the true purpose of the bus ministry. Pastor and Lois vowed they would not allow the bus ministry to stop serving the minority neighborhoods while they were still Pastors of the Church.

As was happening before we left, a large contingent of the Church was withholding their financial support. This was making it more and more difficult to maintain the bus ministry.

The most telling thing about the turmoil in the Church was the spirit of rebellion and anarchy we experienced from the Youth group and bus ministry kids... Remember when I said we would have the buses filled with kids singing praise and worship songs and it was like a choir of angels? Not any longer. The kids were noisy, out of control, and rebellious.

I will NEVER forget an incident that happened during this contentious time. While driving a bus one Wednesday night, I picked up a 13-year-old girl named Lupe from a Hispanic neighborhood. Lupe was a sweet, gentle girl who had been in the bus ministry long before we ever came to Garden City. That night, the atmosphere on the bus was loud and chaotic... *It was out of control.*

I tried to get the kids to sing, but they were too interested in doing anything but singing. As we neared the Church, a scuffle broke out in the rear of the bus. I was forced to pull the bus onto the side of the road to diffuse the situation. I never experienced the kids being so out of control and certainly did not see an outward reason for it. The problems we were experiencing in the Church were not readily apparent to the kids. At least, not that I was aware. Yet, something had to be inciting this uncontrolled and troubling behavior.

As I returned to the driver's seat after diffusing the scuffle, I approached the row with Lupe and some of her friends. She was screaming and out of control like the rest of the kids. Right before I made it to her row, she screamed and threw her head back violently, smashing it into the window next to her seat. Completely to my surprise and horror, the window shattered! The bus may have been old, but the glass should not have broken the way it did. All the kids started laughing and screaming, "AGAIN! AGAIN! AGAIN!"

I lunged towards Lupe with my heart pounding out of my chest, expecting blood, crying, or even worse. Nope. She was *LAUGHING*. There was no blood, and she seemed fine. Chills went down my spine. This was not right, and I could not fathom that it just happened before my eyes. If I hadn't seen it, I would not have believed it. There was something completely wrong, and it had to be spiritual because I could not see any other reason for all of this.

I watched Lupe like a hawk until we arrived at Church and then informed her teacher to keep an eye on her. She never showed any signs of a concussion or other issues. ***This was a physical manifestation of a deeply spiritual issue within the church.***

At about the same time that all this was happening in the ministry we were introduced to a little angel named Jessica. She was a squat, round-faced, melancholy, 3–year–old cherub. She had raven hair with a short 'bowl' cut. She rarely talked, but her melancholy eyes spoke volumes. One look and you could feel the sting of rejection and pain she bore in her infant soul.

She was being fostered by Harvey and Teresa Revere, friends of ours at Church. She was removed from her home because her mother's boyfriend severely beat and hospitalized her on more than one occasion.

The Revere's had several biological children and were currently adopting another. They took-in Jessica because the local social services desperately needed foster parents. This was expedited because the Revere's were already registered foster parents. When Teresa mentioned to Vangie that they might have to give up Jessica due to the current strain on their own family, Vangie's heart melted. After a short discussion, we decided we would apply to be foster parents and provide a home for little Jessica.

The continuous and ongoing need for foster parents made the application process go very quickly. We dealt primarily with a guarded, thirty-something-year-old social worker named Denay Helms. Denay seemed to be an intense girl but based on the job she did on a daily basis, this was probably warranted.

On her first visit to our house, Denay explained that the home study was the major hurdle to receiving a "License" for foster care. However, it turned out to be only about a *two-hour* process. Denay and another gal came to our house, took background information, and then walked through the house. They talked to Brandi and Brittanie and then said they would get back to us after our background checks came back. That was it. We were expecting a much more rigorous vetting process.

About a week later, Jessica was in our arms. I have never seen a child so accepting of new surroundings. We found out this was not the first time she had been remanded to foster care. Most of her short tenure on earth was spent with various foster families. Her poor little ears were malformed from the intense beatings she endured at the hands of her mother's boyfriend.

Denay left us with a pensive little girl, a packet of information, and a phone number to call if we had any issues. She visited us two more times in the next month to check on Jessica. That was it. On the second visit, she said that a judge would never allow Jessica to go back to her mother and that if we were thinking of adoption, it could be a reality.

Jessica firmly wrapped her chubby little arms around all four of our hearts. Brandi and Brittanie immediately accepted her as their sister, and she bonded with them as siblings. It took very little time before she ran to the front door with a huge, heartfelt hug to welcome me home from work each day. She was as natural to our family as if Vangie had given birth to her. She was now our third and youngest child.

Without any warning whatsoever, three months after she became an integral part of our lives and family, a teary-eyed Denay Helms knocked at our door to take Jessica back to her biological mother. It seems a liberal judge decided that she should be returned to her mother and her offending boyfriend. Yes, the same boyfriend who unsuccessfully tried to kill her on previous occasions. ***Apparently, they went to a class that taught them how to be better parents...***

To say that we were devastated would be an insult to our humanity. We fell headlong into mourning for the loss of this precious child in our lives. We were shaken to the core and incensed at a judicial system so screwed up that it would allow this kind of travesty.

We have heard and read many arguments for children like this being returned to their parents. In this case, it was the mother and a boyfriend who had demonstrated multiple times that he could not be trusted and inflicted his anger on the child without restraint. However, *he did attend a class...*

A few weeks after losing Jessica, we saw her in a local grocery store with her biological mother. She reached her arms out and cried for us to take her. It was more than we could bear. It was like having one of our children kidnapped and then seeing her, while being completely helpless to grab her from the offending criminal. I knew then we could not stay in Garden City. Besides losing Jessica, church and work were both going poorly.

A week later, the Church Elder board consisting of The Elgins and their relatives arrived at Pastor and Lois Nelson's house and demanded an IMMEDIATE meeting. It was a little after 9:00 PM, and the sun had already set on the Kansas prairie. Lois immediately called us and asked if we would come over as soon as possible to be with them during this "meeting."

Vangie had just put the kids to bed when Lois called, so it took us a bit to get the kids back out of bed, dressed, and then drive to their house. When we arrived, we were met at the front door by Lois crying and Pastor as pale as a ghost. When Lois answered the door, she immediately wrapped her arms around Vangie and sobbed uncontrollably. She clung tightly to her, swaying slowly back and forth as she wept.

"They did it. They really did it." She blubbered with deep sobs. "They came and told us we were fired and demanded we sign an agreement to quietly leave the area."

I was completely shocked at her words. I looked at Pastor, and he was just sitting, disheveled and with a look of total angst.

He quietly began to speak. "They offered us $10,000.00 to leave the area quietly." He shook his head for a few moments. "Those buzzards learned their lesson from the previous Pastors who started other Churches in the area." He continued to shake his head. "I told them to take their vile, corrupted money and get out of my house. I wanted nothing from them and nothing to do with them."

We remained with them for several more hours. We prayed off and on for peace and direction and then talked about what they would do next. Toward the end of the second hour, Gordon prayed and asked the Lord to forgive the Church Board of Trustees and then told the Lord he would do the same. He broke down and cried as he was praying the prayer. It was only a few moments after his prayer that the heaviness of the evening lifted. We began to widen our conversation and found ourselves laughing at some of the things that had taken place during better times in the past year.

The Nelsons owned a small camping trailer. They decided they would leave the next day and get away from Garden City to clear their heads and make some decisions as to what direction to go. It was now quite late, and the kids were beginning to fuss. We knew we had to take them home to bed. We hugged Pastor and Lois one more time, assuring them everything would be fine, and then we returned home for the evening.

The next morning, at about 9:30, we received a call from Lois. She was very excited and asked if we could come over again. Upon arriving, we found the two of them exuberant and loading their camper. They received a call from a Pastor and old friend of theirs saying a new Church in Mesa, Arizona, opened up and needed a Pastor. He had recommended Gordon and Lois to fill the position!

Gordon and Lois absolutely loved Arizona, and it would put them much closer to their grown children and grandchildren. It seems the Lord had another, better, plan for them. As for us, we just wanted out of there. *Especially now.*

We never returned to First Assembly of God in Garden City after that day. The small amount of time we remained in Kansas found us floating to different Churches, but never committing to any of them. We were devastated at losing Jessica and angry and bitter over what happened with Gordon and Lois. It changed our view of Churches. Tragically, we lost much of our innocence and zeal after our Church experience in Garden City.

During this same period, I was labeled as a religious fanatic at the plant. Besides Don Unger, I was successful in proselytizing another operator named Larry Bastrop. This was a multi-week effort that culminated in him giving me his Book of Mormon. Unfortunately, the religious fanatic label was procured through my UNSUCCESSFUL attempts to lead others into what I considered a saving knowledge of Christ.

My ignorance as to the effect of being someone's supervisor and then compelling them to think a certain way was astounding. They would acquiesce to my mini-sermons in person but, apparently, were far more negative and vocal behind my back. Had these actions happened 30 years later, I probably would have faced legal action due to the secularizing of America that occurred during the subsequent years.

The pinnacle of my zeal at Holcomb Station occurred on a weekend dayshift. An expected and regular 90-car coal supply train arrived at the plant property the previous evening. After entering the plant property, the engineers transferred the train to qualified plant personnel. These coal-handling personnel moved the train through the rotary dumper building when they were ready to unload it. Once emptied, the railroad engineers would return the train to the Wyoming coal fields for reloading.

At about 10:30 Saturday morning, the radio squawked to life. "Coal yard to Shift Supervisor, Coal yard to Shift Supervisor." They virtually never talked to the Shift Supervisor unless they had a serious issue. The coal yard personnel were competent and usually did their jobs with little or no oversight from us. They were in a league of their own and were normally self-sufficient.

I immediately keyed my radio, a bit surprised by their query. "This is the Shift Supervisor. What can I do for you?"

"You can call the cops. We found stowaways on the lead engine. It looks like two guys. We don't want to take any chances with them. Please call the cops to get them out of there." I thought about their request for a few minutes before answering.

"I will be out in a few minutes. Stay out of the engine until I get there."

The coal yard supervisor immediately answered. "We have NO INTENTIONS of getting on the engine. We don't want to mess with these guys." I found it odd they were so apprehensive about this. I never really gave much thought to a situation like this occurring. We certainly never received any training or Management direction for "stowaways."

I went to the parking lot and got into my car. An outside operator had the facility pickup and was busy checking the plant water wells. I didn't want to wait for its return, so I drove my car into the coal yard as close to the locomotives as possible. Two very anxious coal handlers met me. They hurried to my car as I pulled up close to the lead locomotive.

The younger of the two coal handlers blurted loudly, "Did you call the cops?" I slowly opened the door and exited the car.

"No. I will handle this." The situation didn't seem fearful or tense to me. It certainly had absolutely *NOTHING* to do with bravery or courage. I just did not see it as a threatening situation in any way.

The older of the two looked at me with concern and a tinge of anger. "You're nuts, man! I wouldn't touch this with a ten-foot pole unless I had a shotgun in my hand." I still did not feel any reticence, even with his surprisingly fearful demeanor.

I walked to the lead locomotive and climbed the steep steps to the cab. The rhythmic, deep rumble from its idling engine was interrupted by a momentary ear-piercing hiss of air coming from under the locomotive. It would have scared me far worse had I not heard these air blasts many times in the past when the trains were in the yard.

My first real pang of apprehension occurred as I slowly turned the latch and opened the cab door. Sure enough. There were two men who looked to be in their late twenties or early thirties. Both were visibly filthy and wearing rags that were a stretch to call clothing. The taller of the two had hollow, empty eyes with deep, dark circles under them. He did not seem angry or fearful. The other looked terrified and backed up a step or two against the rear of the cab as I entered. He was much shorter than the man directly in front of me.

"What are you guys doing in here?" I asked gently. They looked at each other and then back at me.

"No habla englis."

We stared at each other for a few more moments. It was easy to see they were exhausted. Since it was obvious we couldn't communicate with words, I mimed holding a plate and eating from it. Both of their eyes immediately lit up. The one in front vigorously shook his head yes. I felt peace again. I held the cab door open as I backed out and used my hand to draw them from the locomotive cab. They willingly followed me down the steep steps and to my car.

The coal handlers stood by with a look of total disbelief on their faces. The tallest of the vagabonds sat in the passenger front seat, and the other sat in the passenger-side back seat. It was painfully obvious they had not showered in a while.

At that point, I felt it was the right time to pray. I turned and looked at both men while cupping my hands in front of my mouth, saying, "Hay-suse Christo?" which I knew meant Jesus Christ in Spanish. They both eagerly shook their heads yes.

I prayed a simple prayer of redemption, help, and peace over these men. When we finished, I noticed the man sitting next to me made the Catholic cross on his chest. There was an honest peace in the car. I put the car into reverse and began backing away from the area. I noticed the coal handlers shaking their heads as they walked away.

I drove my two new, down-and-out friends to the main plant and did the mime of eating from a plate again. Again, their eyes lit up. It was easy to see they were very, very hungry. They followed me into the main plant elevator, and we went to the control room. When we walked in, everyone was wide-eyed and looked both angry and frightened.

We had a freezer full of expensive TV dinners for hungry overtime workers that we were obligated to feed. I pulled a couple of them out, showing them to my new friends prior to popping the first one into the microwave. My control room operator, Marion Simmons, urgently motioned me into the control room as the first TV dinner heated.

"What the hell are you doing with those two guys?" His voice was tense and angry.

"I am feeding them. They appear to be half-starved."

I didn't care for Marion's tone or demeanor at that moment. I looked intensely at him and continued, "While they are eating, you can call the Holcomb Sheriff's department and tell them we have two non-English speaking men here. They need to come and process them."

I paused and looked Marion directly in his eyes. "You make darn sure you tell them they are peaceful and non-resisting." He just stared at me with venom in his eyes before picking up the phone. The Sheriff's Department phone number was prominently posted next to the control room desk phone, along with the fire department and ambulance service.

Both men ravenously consumed their TV dinners. There were also some ice-cream bars in the freezer. They seemed to thoroughly enjoy their gourmet dinner and dessert. I was a bit apprehensive about the Sheriff arriving. I was praying under my breath that there would not be an incident of any sort.

Two personnel from the Sheriff's Department arrived in the control room about 30 minutes later. They were cool and collected and did not act aggressively. The wayfarers were stoic and surrendered with no fanfare. They had already showered me with "Gracias, gracias mi amigo" several times. As the Sheriff began to escort them from the control room, the taller of the two gently shook my hand while placing his other hand on my arm. He spoke some words to me in Spanish that I didn't understand, but looking into his eyes, I knew they were decent, thankful words.

All's well that ends well, right? Wrong! Turns out I broke a ton of protocols. In fact, I was pummeled by both Curt and Brad for doing something "completely irresponsible and stupid." I was lectured for bringing interlopers to the control room of an operating facility and endangering my life and the lives of my peers. I was even chastised for not waiting for the operator to return with the company pickup and driving my car into the coal yard!

It didn't matter. In my heart, I was already finished. I suppose they were right, but it didn't affect me. I had already checked out and was done with Western Kansas, *this time in perpetuity.*

Once again, our lives were about to irreversibly change forever. A new chapter in our lives was about to quickly unfold.